strike a new
career deal

"Job security is gone forever. The time is right for ambitious individuals to take control of their own careers."

strike a new
career deal

BUILD A GREAT FUTURE IN THE
CHANGING WORLD OF WORK

Carole Pemberton

FINANCIAL TIMES
PITMAN PUBLISHING

FINANCIAL TIMES
MANAGEMENT
LONDON · SAN FRANCISCO
KUALA LUMPUR · JOHANNESBURG

*Financial Times Management delivers the knowledge,
skills and understanding that enable students,
managers and organisations to achieve their ambitions,
whatever their needs, wherever they are.*

London Office:
128 Long Acre, London WC2E 9AN
Tel: +44 (0)171 447 2000
Fax: +44 (0)171 240 5771
Website: www.ftmanagement.com

A Division of Financial Times Professional Limited

First published in Great Britain 1995
This edition published 1998

© Pearson Professional Limited 1995

ISBN 0 273 63544 1

British Library Cataloguing in Publication Data
A CIP catalogue record for this book can be obtained from the British Library.

10 9 8 7 6 5 4 3 2

Typeset by Avocet Typeset, Brill, Aylesbury, Bucks.
Printed and bound in Great Britain by Bell and Bain Ltd, Glasgow.

The Publishers' policy is to use paper manufactured from sustainable forests.

the author

Carole Pemberton is a research consultant at Sundridge Park Management Centre, working with major UK organisations on issues of career management. She is a trained careers counsellor, who has helped many people to have successful careers. She is also an experienced writer on career issues, contributing to newspapers, human resources magazines and *Cosmopolitan*.

For my mother who has
encouraged all her children to
strike their own career deals

contents •••

Part Two   MAKING IT WORK FOR YOU

"You are tired of hearing that 'there's no such thing as a job for life', as though this is a new reality."

introduction • • •

I'll guess that you've picked up this book because you are concerned as to how you can manage your career in a present and future which appears increasingly unsure. You may have seen able colleagues lose their jobs. Career promises which you thought had been made have not been fulfilled. You are probably like most of the other 24 million workers in this country, experiencing job insecurity. Even if your job isn't immediately vulnerable, the 90s has become a decade of nervousness. Put the pieces together and it is clear that the idea of career is changing. The tactics for getting ahead proposed in the 70s and 80s no longer hold true.

You are undoubtedly working harder than you did five years ago, and yet there may still be no promotion or job move in sight. Already you have discovered that knowing your career goals, identifying your personal strengths and honing your cv are no longer enough to ensure your next job move will bring with it promotion. You have discovered that doing your job well, and committing yourself to the organisation are insufficient to ensure your continued place in it. We have entered a period when redundancy is a professional career norm. The experience of career plateauing can strike a good performer in their 30s, where once it was the preserve of the over 50s who had visibly reduced their career commitment.

How can you as a manager, or professional, male or female, make sense of what is happening and continue to have a sense of career? Is the answer to run even faster? To work harder than your colleagues, to absorb whatever pressures are put on you without complaint, to abandon any idea of balancing your personal and working life? Are these the prices to be paid for retaining a foot on a career ladder, which has fewer and fewer rungs? Should you readjust your career expectations and look to carry on doing what you are presently doing, in the hope that you won't attract attention, and you can ride out the rest of your career in peace? Not a motivating thought if you are only ten years into your career. Or should you simply abandon any thoughts of an organisational career, and trust instead to your own ability to meet your financial needs through selling your time as a self-employed contractor?

All three options are being taken up by individuals. Whether they make personal sense has to be assessed against personality and values differences, lifestyle preferences and, equally importantly, the organisational context. Whatever career management solution you choose has to match against what you need and can offer, and what organisations need and can offer you.

That's why this book is called *Strike a New Career Deal*, because careers in the future are going to be based on a new kind of matching process. If you are tired of hearing that, 'There's no such thing as a job for life', as though this is a new reality, consider whether this has ever been so. What the warning does tell us, is that we can no longer assume that the organisation will want us for as long as we want it. It's a message that's long been understood by manual and unskilled workers, but for professionals it's a new truth. Look at that statement from a different perspective, and it is also telling organisations that they can no longer assume the continued loyalty of their employees. Relationships are going to be based on different sorts of contracting process. It's those different sorts of contracts, and how you can use them to build your career which is the focus of this book.

Just starkly stating that employment security has gone even for the best educated and trained is to simplify the situation. Organisations continue to need the knowledge and skills of the most able, but they are now reconsidering the career deal they can offer and redefining their needs. If your organisation has downsized and delayered (and few have not), it's unlikely they can offer you promotion at the rate you've come to expect. That may well be the reason you picked up this book. But, are there other things which they could offer, which would help sustain your sense of worth, self-confidence and motivation? Or is it simply that organisations can no longer be trusted, and your best strategy is to look after number one, going from job to job constantly monitoring the job market and adding to your cv, while always avoiding commitment – like a jilted lover, who vows that no one is ever going to hurt them again, and plays the field avoiding all ties.

Or let's change the perspective and ask, do you know what you are now willing to offer an employer, and do you know the value they place on the skills which you have? Do you know what you need in order to have a sense of career satisfaction? Has it changed, and can your present employer deliver it?

It's by addressing these issues and honestly appraising both ourselves and the new realities of the workplace, that we can begin to start drawing up new deals, to replace existing ones which have been torn apart.

In reading this book you are being invited to take the risk of looking at the future, and identifying your place in it. If you believe that once the 'feel good factor' returns to the economy, everything will return to how it was you are deluding yourself, and you will find little comfort in these pages. How it was before was only ever a transition. Each successive recession has resulted in the need for less full-time workers. Each major advance in technology from the Industrial Revolution onwards has ultimately led to job losses. Add to this the growth of a global economy, where telecommunications is creating a global labour market, and it becomes impossible to believe that organisations can look as they did even ten years ago. While informed employees can readily recognise business changes, relating them to the implications for our own career options is a more difficult process. Making that link throws up personal uncertainty and discomfort, and so it is tempting to hope that, for us, things will carry on as normal.

I am inviting you to take the risk of looking at the present and future, in order to identify your place in it. I want to help you develop your own new career deal. It may be different from what you expected when you first set out on your career. It may not be what your parents expected for you. Alternatively, it may open up freedoms and satisfactions which have not been on offer to those who have sought a traditional career. It may offer men some of the options which have only been on offer to women, and it may offer women the opportunity of building a career on a more equal basis. It may even offer more fun and personal challenge.

You are part of a transition where the idea of career is undergoing radical change. In working through this book you will be helped to understand what is being left behind, and where you are heading. You will be helped to understand what *you* need in order to be personally satisfied, and directed towards areas where you need to develop.

Career books in the 70s and 80s encouraged us to believe that if we knew ourselves we could achieve anything. They made us feel good, because they placed our destiny in our own hands. This career book is of the 90s, where knowing ourselves is no less important, but knowing the context in which we are operating has never been more important.

You can still have a successful career, but you'll need to spend some time teasing out what you mean by successful, and what you now mean when you talk of career. Accept the challenge of working through your new career deal, and you'll create a career resilience that will sustain you in the whole of your working life.

❝ *Parkinson's Law is dying.* **❞**

part one
•••
the changing context of careers

"When we join an organisation we are each given an employment contract. At the same time, although it's never spoken of, we negotiate a psychological contract."

the way we were

'*They spend their time mostly looking forward to the past.*'
John Osborne

When my mother left school she expected to work as a shop assistant, as had her mother. The fact that she was bright, and creative played no part in her occupational choice. She was the eldest of seven children from a working-class family, leaving school in Liverpool at the beginning of World War Two. Her career goal was to be a window dresser, and career disappointment meant being sent instead to the munitions factory. What need of a window dresser when shop windows were blacked out as security against German bombs?

As her daughter, again the eldest, I left grammar school and went to university – the first of my family to do so. I went with an unquestioning acceptance that it was my right to study, rather than being sent out to work in order to support the family budget. I also had the financial security to do so. As the child of a single parent, the existence of the welfare state provided the funds that made that choice possible. I went to college with an ill-defined sense that a career would follow. Ill defined, because in the family I came from, people did not do jobs that required degrees. As an eighteen year old this did not concern me, because it was obvious that people who went to college ended up with 'good jobs'. There was no concern to choose a vocational degree – simply doing more of what I had been good at at school was assumed to be qualification enough for anything that might follow. What did concern me was how I would recognise a 'good job'. Since it often seemed to follow from a period of travel, I travelled, with the expectation that the journey would develop my self-confidence, and the hope that it would unearth abilities and interests that I had not previously suspected. This exploration would need to happen by my mid-twenties, because by then, I (and my mother) believed, I would need to have sorted myself out. By chance I did. A temporary job in a South African university brought me into contact with students who, despite having every chance to succeed, seemed to have little view of what they wanted to do. I discovered that I enjoyed helping them and returned to the UK with a sense that a job involving careers work could be enjoyable. Had I travelled elsewhere, who knows what the career outcome would have been.

"for all of us our present career perspective has been shaped by the context in which we grew up."

I start with the experience of myself and my mother in order to make the point that for all of us our present career perspective has been shaped by the context in which we grew up. That context shapes the career model we develop, the early working experiences which we are exposed to, and our expectations of the future.

My mother's experience seemed to me to be a terrible denial of her abilities, but to her was all that a working-class girl could aspire to. My experiences will look similarly anachronistic to a reader whose career expectations have been shaped by the 80s and 90s. To graduates I now encounter, who are earnestly comparing MBA programmes, building their cvs while still students, keenly monitoring the financial press and building contacts with a rapier focus, my approach was that of an amateur. To other graduates I meet, who, despite gaining good degrees and determined job search, can only find temporary or unskilled work, my casualness will appal. I was able to stumble towards a career, because in the 1970s the labour market was still expanding, and graduates were a relatively scarce resource. We cannot start to look at our career future, whether we are reading this as an individual with two, ten or twenty years' working experience, without looking to and acknowledging its past, and the context in which it has been grown. Even before we attempt to review that past, we need to recognise that the idea of career is one which has pervaded our society over a very short period of time.

● ● ● Career – where did the idea come from?

Some claim that the word career derives from French *carrière*, a word that has its roots in the word for racecourse, and which, in its present-day form, also means a professional soldier. Others see the roots in the Latin word for road, implying a course over which people travel. In both derivations are clues as to our associations with the idea of career. A career implies a visible way ahead, of winning in a race

"A career implies a visible way ahead, of winning in a race against others."

against others, of defeating opposition, getting to the finishing line in front of the rest. Of course it has gained other connotations: the idea that a career is the preserve of a certain élite of people, professionals and managers, but not a word to be used by plumbers, cleaners or shop assistants. The word was first claimed by those who had a vocation, a lifelong occupation to which they gave their total commitment. As we will see in later chapters that idea is being challenged by new organisational and personal realities, but for now, we need to acknowledge the power of the idea of a lifelong commitment to work.

The concept of career would have been almost unheard of one hundred years ago, outside of a small number of professions. Few of our grandparents would have described their working life in terms of career. For most, talk of work would have been in terms of an exchange of effort for pay. In terms of Maslow's hierarchy of need, for most people working life was an attempt simply to secure their economic means of survival, rather than a means of fulfilling a sense of self. It is in the twentieth century that the concept of career has expanded and with it has come a number of associations now strongly embedded in our psyche.

● ● ● The growth of career

This expansion came with the growth of organisations. In all Western countries, this century has been one in which organisations that started as small family concerns have grown into large corporations through acquisitions and mergers. In the name of efficiencies of scale and protection against competition, companies grew, and as they did so they came to need systems to co-ordinate effort and people to control those systems. Organisations came to be managed, and management was created as a distinct activity.

Being part of management separated the colour of the shirt you wore, the dining room you ate in, and even the toilet you used. A managerial career became the goal of those who wanted to better themselves, but who lacked entrepreneurial ambitions to create their own organisation. The word career is accurately used here, because management became both a vocation and a competitive tournament. The growth of organisations meant not just that managerial activity became a profession, but that a hierarchy of management was created, through which individuals could progress.

The notion of career had a great deal of appeal to those who wanted to achieve more than their parents. It also had appeal to many parents, who while they may have been self-employed, did not encourage their offspring to follow. A career goal within an organisation became to reach the next level of the organisational pyramid by knocking out peers in a competitive joust. Terms such as 'high flyer' were created to describe those who would be given a helping hand up the ladder. Even for those who were not identified stars, there was plenty of room because the ladder had many rungs. When managers in one bank told me that on average they had been promoted every two years in careers which had taken them from early 20s to mid-40s, and that they were now in middle management grades, there was no questioning as to the real nature of these promotions. Promotions had symbolic importance as bolsters of self-esteem, providing access to the increasing symbols of status which the organisation gave as reward. These managers had careers, in which they could expect to continue progressing until their 50s, when it was commonly accepted that promotion would cease. They would be left to sit out their careers until retirement on a career plateau. This event would lead to a reevaluation of the relative importance of work and private life, with a refocusing on externals regarded as the healthiest response. The man who

"The notion of career had a great deal of appeal to those who wanted to achieve more than their parents."

had given his total efforts to the company was now encouraged to take on community responsibilities, to discover the golf course and to mentor younger colleagues.

It was accepted by the organisation that plateauing implied at best a maintenance of performance, and usually a gradual decline. This pattern was accepted, and indeed institutionalised, since rewards were based on length of service rather than performance outcomes. There was recognition for having given committed service over the long term. The same model held true for the professions, who created their own hierarchies stretching from clerk to senior partner. It was equally visible in the public sector, where the growth of the welfare state created new professional activities, and the emergence of public sector management. While the public sector could not provide the financial rewards of the private, the creation of complex hierarchies provided enough subtle distinctions to motivate careerists.

The notion of career, therefore, had a great deal of appeal. Men knew that if they offered loyalty and commitment, and had ability, they were likely to be well rewarded. But what did organisations gain from institutionalising the idea of career? The answer is a great deal.

● ● ● The organisational benefits of career

For large organisations the growth of the idea of career worked to their advantage. They knew that those who did not exit quickly were likely to make a long-term commitment. In the post-war period when the labour market was tight, organisations were growing, and the competitive environment was stable, it made sense to encourage people to tie themselves in, and to discourage them from looking elsewhere. They knew that over time managers developed both an enormous knowledge of the organisation, and an enormous personal investment in it. They could, therefore, rely on continuity, and because of this could plan for succession with confidence. When a departmental head retired there would be obvious candidates who had served long apprenticeships, in readiness for that moment. They also knew they could rely on people to go the extra mile when the pressure was on, and to view that as being part of membership of the company family, rather than worker exploitation. People gave more when needed, because in return they expected the organisation to support them if things got difficult. It may sound as though I am describing some halcyon time, but looked at coolly it was a model of mutual **dealing** which brought a coincidence of interest.

● ● ● The psychological contract – a key career concept

The idea of dealing is central to this book. When we join an organisation, whether in the public or private sector, we are each given an employment contract which lays out the terms and conditions of our employment. At the same time, although it is probably never spoken of we negotiate a **psychological contract** with our new employer. The psychological contract, or deal, contains what we believe we can offer our employer, and what we expect in return. At the same time, the employer has assessed what they can offer us, and what they expect in return. If the process matches, there is a satisfactory deal. It is an exchange made up of intangibles, but it is no less real for that. When the deal ceases to be satisfactory from our side, we know because our feelings and actions change. Suddenly we turn first to the vacancy pages in newspapers, or we feel resentment when we are asked to do more than we think is 'fair'. Where our head was once full of ideas about how we could improve things, now it is filled with negative thoughts about our employer and colleagues. From the employer's side it is even more visible when we are no longer fulfilling the deal they now expect. At its most dramatic we are made redundant. Less dramatically but still often loaded with emotion, we find ourselves sidelined. It becomes obvious that our skills are no longer important, or career promises are no longer talked about.

> **The psychological contract is the exchange deal which the individual and the organisation believes it has with the other**

Consider the career model, which I have suggested operated in the second half of the twentieth century until the 1980s. For an employee who sought a career as a professional or manager, the deal could look like this:

I offer ...	The organisation expects ...
My loyalty.	Loyalty.
In-depth knowledge of this organisation.	Staff with a deep understanding of how business is done here.
Acceptance of bureaucratic systems which will define my rate of progress.	A willingness to build a career slowly through a a defined system.
A willingness to go beyond the call of duty when required.	An 'organisation man' who puts the organisation before outside interests.
I expect ...	**The organisation offers ...**
To have job security.	Job security.
Regular pay increases.	Regular pay increases based on length of service, rather than performance measures.
Recognition for length of time given.	Status and rewards for length of service.
To have my experience taken account of.	Respect for experience.

In this example the offers and expectations clearly match. There is a mutually satisfactory deal, which explains why so many managers were content to be 'organisation men'. The term is an accurate one, both because individuals identified themselves strongly with an organisation, but also because to be a manager was almost always to be male. Women working in organisations at that time would identify a very different sort of deal, where the exchange was often far from balanced. In the example above, there is something notable about the nature of the exchange, it has a strong sense of **relationship**, a sense of expectations and mutual understandings growing over time. It was **relational**, building the interdependencies that keep people together through good and bad times. The organisation tolerated performance decline towards the end of a career because the individual had built up a bank of good will earlier in their career. Individuals would give their all because they believed the organisation would in turn look after them.

What may sound like rosy-hued nostalgia was in reality a mutually satisfying contract, satisfactory because it matched the business needs of the organisation, at a time when conditions were largely stable and expanding. It also matched the personal interests of individuals who had learnt from the career insecurities experienced by their own parents, as children of the 1930s and 40s, that finding a 'good job' in a 'good firm' and sticking with it was smart career management.

● ● ● What was your deal?

The idea of the career deal doesn't only apply to our parents and grandparents, it also applies to you. When you entered the labour market and made your first career choice you negotiated a deal, even if you were unaware of it at the time. Consider the first job you ever did:

What did you believe you offered?

- an openness to learn?
- specialist expertise?
- long-term commitment?
- new ideas?
- a willingness to work twenty-four hours a day?

What did you expect in return?

- a planned career?
- an opportunity to learn from experts?
- the chance of making a lot of money quickly?
- rapid promotions?
- experience that would help your cv?
- an assurance that your future would be secure?

None of the above may apply to you, but it is certain that you brought both offerings and expectations to the negotiating table. These offerings could have been as simple as a willingness to do whatever they wanted, in the expectation that they would give you sufficient money to enable you to clear your debts or buy a car. It was a negotiation process that was probably unexpressed, or at least not in these terms. As unimportant as that first job may now seem, it's important to be clear about the deal you first entered, because it will help you in understanding the state of your present deal, and the deal which you want to work towards in the future. Answer these same questions for yourself:

When I entered the job which was the beginning of my career:

offered ...
●
●
●
●
●
●

expected ...
●
●
●
●
●
●

Now change the angle of your viewfinder and consider, what did your first employer offer and expect from you? They may have offered:

● A fast-track scheme for those identified as high potential.
● The only source of employment in your locality.
● A well-known name that imbued status to those who worked for them.
● A learning model based on throwing people in at the deep end and forcing them to learn quickly.
● Planned development so that experience was gained gradually, without risk taking.

In return they will have had their own expectations. These could have been:

● To get as much as possible out of eager new entrants, with no expectation of their staying long.
● To induct you into the company way, so that you were quickly shaped by the organisation.
● That you would not be of any great value until you had served your apprenticeship, and acquired professional qualifications.
● That you would earn your keep from day one.
● Total commitment to the exclusion of your personal life.

Again these offerings and expectations may not accurately assess what the organisation dealt you, so consider for yourself what was their hand?

They offered ...	They expected ...
●	●
●	●
●	●
●	●
●	●

When you consider the level of match between what you offered and expected and what they offered and expected, how does it now look? Was there a mutual matching process, with a sense of both sides seeking a **relational** contract, a desire to commit for the foreseeable future? Or was there a matching process based on a more pragmatic assessment of mutual need? In this case the deal was **transactional**, where both sides sought a direct exchange, with no commitment beyond the immediate. Did you sign on to an organisation which hired and fired but gave valuable working experience and high rewards? An offering which matched with an individual who wanted to get on quickly, learn rapidly and move on. Or was it even more directly transactional: they offered a job and you needed one; they expected you to turn up on time, and you were happy to clock on?

> **"Deals can come in many forms, the only requirement for mutual satisfaction is that neither side feels it is being exploited."**

● ● ● Why transactions become relations

Deals can come in many forms, the only requirement for mutual satisfaction is that neither side feels it is being exploited. While I have focused on the relational contract, as one which has marked managerial careers, you may disagree. Your assessment of your early working life may be that it has been strictly transactional. For those who place a relatively low importance on career in their early working years, transaction is all that is sought. The pattern of job moves among professionals and managers in their early years suggests that it is highly likely to have been transactional. Those who get on quickest do so by moving around, by acquiring a range of experiences in a number of organisations, ensuring that each move brings promotion and a higher salary. The evidence also suggests that for most people at some point the pattern changes. It may be because of growing family or personal commitments. It may because of finding an organisation that feels comfortable. It may be because relocation loses its appeal, or it may simply be that the external labour market loses its buoyancy. At some point, however, for most people, expectations of the deal shift in the direction of a desire for a more relational contract. As we will see in the next chapter, this internal shift may not match with the shift occurring in the negotiating partner.

At this point, I want to bring you forward to your present employer, to consider the deal which you believe you negotiated when you joined. However recently or long ago you took up employment, answer for yourself the same four questions. The answers you give will be important for moving into Chapter 2. When you joined your **present employer**:

What did you believe you offered them?	What did you expect of them?
●	●
●	●
●	●
●	●
●	●
What did they offer you?	**What did they expect of you?**
●	●
●	●
●	●
●	●
●	●

Listed in this way, does the deal seem transactional or relational? Does it seem balanced or weighted in one party's favour? In answering these questions you may have already recognised a change in the deal between the time when you joined and now. The change may be in you, in that your expectations have altered, but equally it could be in the organisation. Similarly, offerings may have changed for one or both of you. Recognising those changes is important to building a new career deal.

Before moving on to the present, there is one further element of our understanding of career that we need to recognise: the power of the idea of being matched to a career.

● ● ● Careers guidance: the attempt to make a good match

If you received careers guidance while at school or in college it is likely that it followed a model, which attempted to match you to a job. You may have filled in questionnaires which asked about your interests, abilities and values. You were probably asked not only what you were good at, but also what was important to your view of yourself. Would you, for example, be happier helping others, or making a personal statement through your creativity? There may have been computer programs which analysed your views and produced a list of suitable occupations. Unstated in these discussions was a belief that this initial choice of job would define the rest of your working life. A choice of social work would shape a career which built on that initial training – which implied you would never head up an advertising agency. An apprenticeship as a trainee lawyer would, if successful, end with your gaining a partnership and not a sales directorship. Initial job choices were seen as important for those who aspired to a career. Why was this?

An important influence on these beliefs was the context of careers help. When I trained as a careers counsellor in the 1970s, the prevailing models which guided my efforts were those of two Americans, Donald Super and Eli Ginzberg, who in the 1950s defined the choice of career as a process of personal maturation. This meant in practice:

● In childhood we fantasise about jobs – I'd like to be a ballet dancer or I'd like to be a train driver are accepted as career ambitions, although repeated ten years later they may cause parental alarm.

● In early adolescence we start to link our interests and sense of what we are good at to ideas. I am good at physics, I'll be a space scientist. I like animals, I'll work as a dog handler.

● In later adolescence and early adulthood we explore options based on a fuller knowledge of ourselves, and a greater sense of economic and social realities. Parental influences and expectations are often strong shapers at this stage. A graduate with a degree in economics is more likely to test out working for a bank than to join a dance company; another graduate with a high social concern will try out nursing or social work.

● By mid-twenties we have, if mature, established our career choice. The economics graduate may have discovered that banking was not for her and found her place as a business journalist. The nurse may have rejected medicine, but involved himself in project work with a charity. For those who felt at ease with their first choice, the process of career building will have begun with the first promotion. For those who have not yet made a career choice, the pressure of expectation to do so starts to build.

● The 30s and 40s are periods for further establishing the chosen career, with success being judged by the rate of promotions.

● The 50s are for maintaining what has been achieved.

● The mid-50s onwards are a time for performance decline and career deceleration until the finishing line of retirement is reached.

● ● ● The old career models don't work

It is apparent that the career model which Super and Ginzberg defined no longer matches with the later career stages. Relatively few managers and professionals now wait to collect the gold clock at 65, but the pressures to conform to the early career stages remain strong. Yet this model of careers guidance was as much a product of its time as were the relational contracts of the 1950s, 1960s and 70s. The expectation that we should exper-iment a little before making a firm commitment, which we would stick to for the rest of our working lives, was drawn from research work with white male American college students in the 1950s. This group was not only an élite, it was an élite at a particular moment in time. Following World War Two, US industry was rapidly expanding, and in the aftermath of war, the value placed on the traditional nuclear family was high. It made absolute sense for middle-class males to aspire to an early career choice, which would allow them to support a non-working wife and family and to commit themselves to an organisational career. It was through committing to one organisation that aspirations were most likely to be met.

As we will see in later chapters, the job-match model of careers is no longer appropriate for the conditions of the 1990s, but neither is a career model based on early establishment as the only mature career goal. It is a model which has long worked against the interests of those who cannot match it because they entered the labour market later in life, or switched careers. It has helped create the idea of age norms for reaching certain levels in the organisation. An individual who has not reached the grade 'on time' is then judged to have failed by both themselves and their peers. A woman who starts her career in earnest after childrearing is denied the chance of ever reaching the top; the schoolteacher who switches to accountancy in his 30s does so in the knowledge that they can never make partner.

Careers guidance, as much as career contracting, is the product of its time. We need to recognise these realities if we are to give ourselves permission to define a career future that may be different from that which we have grown to expect. We also need to accept the idea of career as in permanent redefinition, if we are to take full advantage of what may now be possible.

Remember

☐ Careers always exist in the context of their time. That context is economic, social and political. What we have come to see as the norm is only a transition point in the evolution of working patterns.

☐ Our model of career has been drawn on conditions that existed in the latter half of the twentieth century. These are conditions which are rapidly changing.

☐ All satisfactory working relationships are based on a process of psychological contracting or dealing between individuals and organisations. The deal is made up of both what an organisation can offer us and what they expect in return, and what we offer an organisation and expect in return. The deal is usually unspoken, but we know when it is has been violated.

☐ For many people, the nature of the deal they have sought is relational, that is, a sense of mutual commitment that mirrors many of the elements of a satisfying personal relationship.

☐ For people in their early career, the deal has often been transactional, a straight exchange of effort for pay. The transactional deal has not traditionally marked the careers of managers and professionals.

☐ Our career models have been shaped by the idea of establishing a career identity in early adulthood, and then building on that identity. Career switches and late entry have not been markers of career success. That model was based on conditions of organisational growth and social stability that are disappearing.

" *Leanness is in danger of becoming anorexia.* **"**

2

the way it is

'*People do realize that job security is gone, but many don't realize what it's been replaced by.*'
Homa Bahrami

The career deal of the past is gone, and its passing is being mourned in canteens, around photocopiers and wherever those who knew a different time gather to talk. Even if strategists would now argue that the old deal undermined business competitiveness, for many employees the old deal worked pretty well. Not that anyone spoke in those terms at the time, it was assumed to be the natural order of things. An annual pay rise was as preordained, as was a permanent work contract and a 35-hour week. If we are now to make sense of where the idea of career is moving, we need to examine what has been happening to organisations to change the deal. What has undermined the sense of career derived from your early working years, or from observation of your parents?

> **"The career deal of the past is gone, and its passing is being mourned in canteens, around photocopiers and wherever those who knew a different time gather to talk."**

● ● ● What's been happening?

Ask people to describe what has been happening to their organisation over the last few years, and a litany of change drops out:

- Greater competition than ever before.

- The removal of regulations that restricted competition and provided a measure of protection.

- The emergence of global competitors who can do the work more cheaply.

- A need to get products and services to the market quicker than ever before.

- Information technology doing jobs more efficiently than the humans who once owned those jobs.

- Information technology giving information to staff that was once the preserve of managers.

- Managers taking on tasks that used to be done by their secretaries.

- Information technology creating a global network so that expertise and labour can be located anywhere in the world.

- The movement of organisations from the public to the private sector.

- A reduction in the autonomy of the public sector with the outsourcing of services and competitive tendering.

● ● ● The global marketplace

In short, the context in which work is carried out has been transformed. Who would have thought that Korea and Taiwan would be seen as major manufacturing competitors; that India would carry out software design for IBM; that the former Soviet Union would be a source of conceptual expertise in the design of computer hardware; or that local refuse would be collected by a Spanish company. The threat being posed by emerging economies is not just that they can provide cheap labour for unskilled work, it's that they can also do skilled work well.

Sir James Goldsmith, writing in *The Times* in March 1993, assessed that there are four billion people entering the world market in countries such as China, Indo-China, Bangladesh and the former Soviet Union. People who are underemployed, and who will accept wages 90 per cent less than their European counterparts. While that labour pool explains the rapid disappearance of unskilled work in the UK, it is only half the story. More threatening to those who have defined themselves as careerists is the availability of a global skill base. Innovation in telecommunications and political change are bringing into the labour supply hundreds of millions of people who are educated, and motivated to take on highly skilled jobs in a world market. Companies such as BT, BA and IBM are using staff in developing countries to do skilled technical work that can be transmitted back to the UK via satellite connection. The belief that Britain has the best education system in the world is challenged by countries such as Singapore and Korea, where the percentage of graduates is now higher than that of the UK and where degrees are in subjects which are directly applicable to manufacturing, design and business management.

Faced with this destabilisation of the business environment, companies had to take action in order to ensure survival. While they saw the need for regeneration and adaptability, they pushed up against financial pressures which have not shown such willingness to flex:

● Shareholders who expect the same or an improved return on dividend year on year.

● Financial institutions who primarily offer short-term funding, and do not see themselves in the long-term alliances with business that mark the relationship between finance and industry among competitors such as Japan and Germany.

● City institutions which focus on maximising return through the international circulation of money, rather than through investment in British industry.

●●● The human consequences of business change

Organisations were already finding themselves facing growing competition, with only limited help from the City, when they were hit from behind by recession and with it the collapse of UK consumer demand. In their need to act in order to survive against this onslaught, most adopted the same strategies of controlling costs, in order both to preserve the bottom line and keep products and services competitively priced. Even if real growth was minimal, cost controls enabled them to stay in business through:

● Making operations more efficient through the use of inform- ation technology.
  Consequence: job losses.

● Restructuring the organisation to maximise output from human and capital resources.
  Consequence: job losses.

● Reducing staffing costs.
  Consequence: job losses and outsourcing.

● Looking to match the workforce with patterns of demand.
  Consequence: job losses, creation of part-time jobs in place of full-time and outsourcing.

● Questioning the need for managers.
  Consequence: job losses, reduction of organisational hierarchies and an increase in demands made on all staff who remain.

● Increasing the importance of small business units over the corporate centre.
  Consequence: job losses at the centre and increased per- formance demands on business units.

● Outsourcing of services voluntarily, or as a result of com- pulsive competitive tendering.
  Consequence: job losses and changed working contracts for those who supply the outsourced labour force.

While your organisation may not have taken all the decisions suggested above, it is certain that they now operate in a way which is significantly different to ten or even five years ago. If you are to make sense of those changes, the first step is to recognise their existence.

> **Ask yourself:**
> What actions has my organisation taken in recent years in order to maintain itself?
> ●
> ●
> ●
> ●
> ●

What have been the human consequences of those actions?
-
-
-

In answering those questions it will have become transparent that the nature of the career deal on offer has changed. The assumptions on which you built your early career can no longer be taken for granted. For many managers, the career deal that is now operating looks like this:

Present career deal

I offer ...	They expect ...
A willingness to work whatever hours are needed in order to do the job.	Whatever hours are needed in order to do the job.
An acceptance of change in what I do, and how I do it.	Acceptance of change.
An acceptance that my role takes on more challenges each year, without any promise of promotion.	Taking on more responsibilities without expecting promotion.
A willingness to learn.	Self-development.

They offer ...	I expect ...
A job for as long as my skills meet with their business need.	A level of job security that allows for some future planning.
Stress.	To be stressed, but to hide it.
Pay linked to performance.	A level of pay which increases annually in recognition of the value of my increased contribution. Some recognition for the fact that I bring years of experience to this role.
Greater responsibilities at an earlier age.	Responsibility, but with sufficient support that the challenge is stretching not stressing.

Look at this deal against that of the past, and there are significant differences. The idea of the contract as being **relational** is gone, at least from the organisation's side. In its place is one based on **transaction**. Employees who have spent less time with the company find this shift less difficult to accept than do those who have a history to undo. It's not just that the deal is transactional, it's also that it is perceived as unequal. If in legal terms a contract is made when an offer is accepted, the acceptance of these offers is often reluctant and sometimes coerced.

● ● ● What's your deal?

The inequality of the deal has been levered by the economic conditions of the 1990s, at a time when the conditions of the labour market have given organisations an upper hand. They have been able to ignore the emotional impact of the new deal, because employees see themselves as having few alternatives. How many times has the answer to complaints about the pressure of work been, 'You should be glad you've still got a job'? Before we consider the consequences of dealing in this way, and there are consequences both for the organisation and individuals, you need to recognise the deal to which you are currently party. Look at your present working situation and identify:

What do I offer?	What do they expect?
●	●
●	●
●	●
●	●
●	●
What do they offer?	**What do I expect?**
●	●
●	●
●	●
●	●
●	●

Acknowledging the deal in this way allows you to recognise both what has changed for you and the organisation since you first joined, but also how satisfied you are with the present contract. Has the contract shifted from relational to transactional, or was it always a straight exchange of skill for pay? Does your organisation mirror the offers and expectations I have outlined, or are the conditions operating on your business so different from those acting on large UK companies that your contract is unchanged, or has even moved in the direction of relational contracting? Those working in small, start-up enterprises or a rapid response FMCG company may find the deal operating in different ways to that of a newly privatised utility or a deregulated finance company. If your organisation has bucked the general economic trend, you may see the deal very differently from those organisations who are attempting to revitalise themselves in order to match competition.

There is no single blue print, but what is important is to recognise how you are presently contracting. It is only through realistically facing what is, rather than yearning for a past that has gone, that we can start to move forward. In drawing up your present deal you are making explicit to yourself a contract which is largely unspoken. In making explicit the shifts it also becomes easier to relate the feelings which are surrounding your present career.

● ● ● Feelings about the present deal

When asked to describe the feelings associated with their present deal, managers and professionals with whom I work are vociferous:

● It makes me angry.

● It's unfair.

● It's exploitation.

● It's demotivating.

● It makes me cynical about this company.

● It makes me want to escape at the first opportunity.

● It makes me feel I have no choices, since I am 45 with two kids and a mortgage to support.

● It's affecting morale.

- I don't have a career anymore.
- It's making me dread coming to work each day.
- Roll on early retirement.

The underlying theme of their comments is a sense of **powerlessness**, a sense of there being no escape route and no negotiating hand with which to change the dynamic. Challenging that sense of powerlessness and transforming it through working with new realities is the key to making a more satisfactory career deal. Before we can do that, we need to look at the whole picture, and not just to focus on our own feelings of entrapment.

● ● ● Organisations have to do more than control costs

Senior managers have taken decisions, which many have found personally difficult, in the name of staying in business. Staying in business is not a sufficient goal. No organisation can sustain its future unless it is also constantly innovating. It is estimated that no organisation can have more than a six-month lead on its competitors, before it needs to make another leap forward in order to stay ahead in the race. If you want evidence of this look at products as diverse as computer hardware and toothpaste. The constant developments in hardware capacity are driven as much by small-scale companies like Dan, as by large scale manufacturers like Dell and Compaq. The small operators have refused to know their place, and now drive the large operators to continuous improvement. As customers we are the winners. Or consider Arm and Hammer baking soda toothpaste. Launched in the UK in 1994 as the toothpaste which left you with a 'fresh from the dentist feeling of clean', it was priced above its well-established competitors. Within six months its impact on the market was such that each of the major toothpaste manufacturers has launched their own version. Yet the product grew not out of a company with a track record in dental care

"No organisation can sustain its future unless it is also constantly innovating."

products, but from a US company which sold a home baking aid. They were able to bring innovation to the dental care market because they defined their core competence as the application of the properties of baking soda, rather than the improvement of cake baking. When I visited the USA in 1995, they had moved on to launch an antiperspirant based on the properties of baking soda. In six months' time they will need to be looking for another application of that core compet -ence.

> **"Every company knows that its real future relies on the ability of the staff to 'know beyond' the present into the future, and to give of their best."**

The rate at which new products and services appear and are accepted, like baking soda toothpaste and personal computers, or rejected, like most new food product launches, emphasises the point that cost competitiveness and cost control are insufficient competitive weapons. Every company knows that its real future relies on the ability of the staff to 'know beyond' the present into the future, and to give of their best. That willingness to 'know beyond' is as relevant to a social services department looking to provide services for a changing demographic base, as it is for a soft drinks company that wants to expand its market by producing a product which adults will choose in preference to alcohol. That ability to harness the capacity of people to 'know beyond' is the real meaning of the glibly repeated phrase that 'people are our most important assets'.

●●● The real meaning of people as assets

In the 1990s the term human assets has become derided. It has come to imply a piece of capital investment to be acquired or divested at the whim of the owner of that capital. The relationship between employer and employee has been compared to that of a plantation owner and slave. It's an appealing analogy because it matches with the mood of cynicism in the workplace, but if we shift our perspective we may discover that the human asset has more career power than it currently realises. Consider company X, a long-established organisation which has been hard hit by business changes. It has now set out a vision statement that is far removed from its present place in the marketplace. In order to move towards its goals, it needs to make the most of its human assets.

Company X has a need to:

- compete effectively day to day
- develop better quality products more quickly then ever before
- attract and retain the best talent available
- get more effort out of those staff who remain
- move into new markets.

Company X has employees who:

- are exhausted by repeated reorganisations
- have seen able colleagues made redundant and fear that they will be next
- have learnt that the best survival tactic is to keep your head down and hope it all goes away
- have discovered that small acts of sabotage give a temporary sense of satisfaction that evens up the feelings of powerlessness
- have given up on the idea of career.

What bets on company X coming up with worldbeating products and services and repeatedly outstripping their main competitor in Asia Pacific? The truth is that having a career deal which is perceived as inequitable acts against the company's long-term interests. It's a message that's starting to be recognised. Consider the outcry that marked a 1994 presentation by senior BT managers. It was expected to be a public PR presentation of record profits and growing internationalisation. It could be expected that there would be a regretful acknowledgement of the one third of employees who had been shed since 1990, together with an affirmation that the organisation was now 'lean and mean' enough to compete worldwide. Instead there was a boiling over of employee emotion as manager after manager, across levels and age groups, railed against their continued sense of job insecurity, the disappearance of pride in working for the company, and a lack of trust in the organisation. This furore was followed shortly afterwards by a letter to the company newsletter arguing that the company was failing to deliver quality and was losing customers, because the drive to

"Job security is leading to 'presenteeism', a fear of being absent in case it marks your redundancy card."

short-term results was making managers too frightened to tell unpalatable truths. Leanness was in danger of becoming anorexia. It is surely no coincidence that not long afterwards the company made a public statement that no further compulsory redundancies were planned.

● ● ● Security is relative

Job insecurity, according to stress expert Professor Cary Cooper, is leading to 'presenteeism', a fear of being absent in case it marks your redundancy card. A concern to be present is very different from a desire to be in the present. Economist Will Hutton assesses that alongside the 30 per cent of society which are disadvantaged because they have lost or are unable to work, there is a further 30 per cent who are insecure because of their relationship with the labour market. These are people who are in casual, part-time or fixed-term contracts. That leaves 40 per cent who he sees as privileged. These are full-time employees and the self-employed who have held their jobs for over two years. If you are in the privileged category, you may feel his assessment is over generous. Or is it that our expectations of job security have shifted? The manager who told me that he had reasonable job security, because his job was secure for the coming year, was using a very different measure than his father would have applied.

● ● ● Are you a survivor?

The story is not confined to the UK. David Noer, a consultant working for the Center for Creative Leadership in North Carolina, speaks of those who are still occupying managerial and professional jobs as 'survivors'. You might expect that they feel relief at still having a job, but in his experience they share many of the feelings of those who survive manmade or natural disasters:

● They ask themselves 'why me, in what way am I any different to my colleagues who lost their jobs?'

● They feel numb and apathetic.

● They constantly think about how life was before.

● Their goals are reduced to simply getting through the day.

> **"Simply surviving is not in itself enough to give us a sense of personal worth, or the motivation to create a new future."**

Simply surviving is not in itself enough to give us a sense of personal worth, or the motivation to create a new future.

When Peter Herriot and I looked at managers who had survived so far in their companies, we found four types of response:

Get ahead

Those who feel that, despite the changes and delayerings, they still want and expect to get ahead of the rest and to scramble up the career ladder. They may secretly believe that redundancies have got rid of 'dead wood' ahead of them, and that the organisation is now a better place for people of ability (like them).

Get safe

Those who are bruised by what has happened, and who believe that the best policy is to try and hang on to doing what they are already doing. The aim is to avoid risk taking and being noticed. The only goal is to see things out until early retirement.

Get out

Those who are looking to get out at the first opportunity. Research Group BDI assessed in November 1994 that 40 per cent of employees currently fall into this group. Their reasons for wanting out are not primarily financial. They often report being bored, and having been left too long in the same place. According

to Ray Eccles of BDI, 'job satisfaction, lack of c
and management style', are making large nu
keen to escape.

Get even

These people feel betrayed by the changes they are ssing.
They see the values to which they were attracted being cast
aside, and they also assess that they have limited opportunities
in the external labour market. In a situation where they feel
trapped, their only satisfaction comes from attempting to
undermine change. Whether it's making false expense claims,
wiping data off their computer, withholding information that
could affect decision making, or leaking company documents to
the press, the goal is the same: temporarily to gain a sense of
control in a deal which they now see as working against them.

As human responses, each of these positions are
understandable, you may even recognise yourself as occupying
one of these categories. They each fall into the 'fight or flight'
responses to threat. Consider them not from your own point of
recognition, but from the perspective of an organisation who has
made major changes to its workforce in the last few years in the
belief that they are now better equipped to innovate, respond
quickly and deliver quality. It now finds itself with a workforce
who:

● When the labour market opens up, will be looking to exit.
  Consequence: loss of talent.

● Seek safety and are unlikely to take the risk of offering new
  ideas, since they may be rejected.
  Consequence: waste of brain power.

● Seek revenge and look to undermine whatever policies the
  organisation attempts to introduce.
  Consequence: wasted energies.

● Believe they can still forge ahead even though the reality is
  reduced promotion opportunities.
  Consequence: disillusionment.

Looked at together, the UK workplace does not look well placed
to meet the challenges which are facing it. How does this help
you as an individual, since one reading could be that things can

get worse if we are so emotionally mismatched with our organisation's new agenda? I believe it can help you. The recognition that there is a gap between the expectations of performance delivery, and the reality of current career attitudes is the foundation upon which a new career deal can begin to be built. Skilled and able individuals are not as powerless as they have assumed themselves to be in recent years. The words are carefully chosen, because a satisfactory career deal is not an open offer to all. Skill and ability are the key to changing the present contract, together with a recognition of the new forms of organisation which are emerging from the debris of large hierarchies.

We will address both elements in the next chapter.

● ● ● Your career is now within you and not in the hands of an employer

We are fooling ourselves if we believe that the past will return and that when the 'feel good factor' returns to the UK economy, layers will be reinstated, career paths will be regravelled and managerial status will be restored. The changes I have described are shaping a business environment that is demanding constant transformation. Those who look to discover the size of the new organisational pyramid will find instead an organisational amoeba which will change shape to deal

"A meaningful sense of career now has to be placed within the individual."

with whatever obstacle is in its way, dividing whenever necessary. From a career perspective it means the direct link between career success and organisation has been broken. A meaningful sense of career now has to be placed within the individual. Each of us must define what we want, and how we can achieve it; what we can offer and what we expect. We also need to recognise that we are not powerless. The future of organisations still rests on people, and getting the best from

"The future of organisations still rests on people, and getting the best from them."

them. The present deal feels out of balance, but it is as much in the interest of organisations to reconsider how they transact with us, as it is for us to each ensure our career resilience. By looking at what the future is bringing, we can start to redefine our own career deal.

Remember

☐ UK organisations faced by deregulation, global competition, a global labour force and changing customer expectations have reshaped in the last ten years. Reorganisation has taken apart the career systems which looked after those in professional and managerial roles and wiped out the career assumptions of the past.

☐ The strategies of cost control and cost competitiveness have meant job losses for experienced and talented individuals. Those that remain report a range of emotional responses, all of which equate with a sense of powerlessness.

☐ The career deal which presently operates is seen by many as a strict transaction between two parties who have little emotional commitment to each other.

☐ The deal seems to be heavily weighted in the organisation's favour because of prevailing economic conditions, which have reduced employees' labour market power.

☐ Looked at from the longer term need of organisations to maximise the creativity of their knowledge base, present feelings of insecurity and demotivation act against those interests.

☐ Equating career with vertical progression no longer describes the experience of many individuals. There is a need for new more individualised definitions, which also match with the realities of the workplace.

"Organisations will continue to have a business and social importance, but they will bear a stronger resemblance to a tent, which can be pitched and then moved on, than to a fixed monument to past success."

the way things are going to be: the organisation's view

'There are good reasons for suggesting that the modern age has ended. Many things indicate that we are going through a transitional period, when it seems that something is on the way out and something else is painfully being born. It is as if something were crumbling, decaying and exhausting itself, while something else, still indistinct, were arising from the rubble.'
Vaclav Havel

The sign on the wall of the Professor of Economics, announcing 'the future is not what it was', warned both himself and his students of the dangers of attempting prediction. The future is always a complex amalgam of the foreseeable, the visible but unrecognised and the unknowable. It is the interaction which can lead to unpredictable outcomes: chaos theory in action. Only ten years ago we were being told of the forthcoming leisure society, where the assumption of adequate financial provision for all would lead us to share out work and buy back the time that had once been sacrificed in the search for career. We would develop satisfying portfolio careers combining paid and unpaid work, and plan our lives around creating a balance between work and leisure. It was a model based on an assumption of power lying in the hands of individuals.

"*the future is not what it was.*"

● ● ● The new meaning of a leisure society

We only have to look back at the past ten years to see how an emerging trend toward more flexible patterns of working was badly misinterpreted. Instead of having created more satisfying lives, where work is but one element, we now have, as Charles Handy now recognises, half the people working twice as hard and producing three times the output.

"half the people working twice as hard and producing three times the output."

Those in work are working longer hours than ever before. UK managers now have the dubious honour of working longer hours than any of our European partners. At the same time we have created a society in which three million people are without work and, if they have been out of work for more than one year, have only a five per cent chance of finding a job in the immediate future. A leisure society has come to mean total leisure for those with no work, and no leisure for those with work: until their 100,000 hours of working life are used up in middle age. The economic pressures of the 1990s have placed power in the hands of organisations, who have applied the concept of flexibility very differently. That experts can get it so wrong is warning against trying to fix the future, but it's a risk we have to take if we are to understand what is shaping organisational decision making, and the expectations they are likely to have of employees in the future. By understanding the organisational mind set, we will be better placed to start considering the career deal which is going to be right for us.

● ● ● Labour market trends

Government projections tell us that by the end of the century 1.6 million more people will be in work, as a result of the creation of new jobs. The numbers themselves are of less importance than the distribution of those jobs: 1.5 million will be in service industries, compared with an increase of less than 0.5 million in distribution and construction, and a loss of 0.5 million in primary and manufacturing industries. The trend towards employment in service industries begun in the 1980s will continue. Already 45 per cent of jobs are in the service sector, while manufacturing, construction and primary industries together now only account for 30 per cent. These government predictions are confirmed by the CBI, which reports that from 1993–4 300,000 extra jobs were created: 125,000 of which were in distribution, hotels and restaurants, and 190,000 in banking, finance and insurance. To rub further salt into manufacturing wounds, during the same period manufacturing saw a further drop of 10,000. Manufacturing was not alone however, the public sector and the privatised utilities also showed a decline. The future in one sense will be like the past, the employment themes of the last ten years will continue apace.

Just saying where jobs will be is insufficient. We also need to know what those jobs will be. In 1992, Amin Rajan made two important distinctions in assessing where new jobs will be:

● Jobs which will either increase or decrease in their numbers.

● Jobs which will either increase or decrease in their skill level.

Put together he produced a model, which is supported by government projections.

Numbers and skills changes in occupations groupings

Numbers increasing

	Group 3	Group 1	
Skills decreasing	Secretarial occupations (part time) Junior clerks (part time) Recreational occupations (part time) Personal services occupations (part time) Security occupations (part time)	Managers and administrators Engineers and scientists Associate professionals Health and educational professionals Multiskilled crafts Sales and marketing Security	Skills increasing
	Group 4	**Group 2**	
	Junior draughtsperson Single skilled craftsperson Operatives Unskilled occupations Manual occupations	Multiskilled clerks Supervisors Secretarial occupations Recreational services Personal service occupations	

Numbers decreasing

The issue is not just where are jobs going to be, it's also what are the skill requirements of those jobs. The prediction that most

"The issue is not just where are jobs going to be, it's also what are the skill requirements of those jobs." new jobs will be women's jobs takes on a different aspect when it is likely that most of those jobs will be part time and low pay. However, deskilling is only part of the picture, what Amin Rajan is also arguing is that there will be skilled jobs for which the demand will increase. His analysis is reinforced by the Institute of Employment Research, which has put percentage figures on the trends. They predict that between 1993–2001, there will be an increase in demands for certain categories of employees:

Managers and administrators	
Corporate managers and administrators	24%
Science and engineering professionals	23%
Managers/proprietors in agriculture and services	11%
Professionals	
Health professionals	13%
Teaching professionals	14%
Other professional occupations	43%
Associate professionals and technical staff	
Science and engineering associate professions	15%
Health associate professionals	0%
Other associate professionals	30%

Such predictions immediately create a problem. They seem to suggest that managerial jobs which were removed in the name of efficiency are going to be reinstated. While such analysis suits the cynic in us, it is not an answer. It is more likely that our definition of management will alter. Many more will be involved in managerial work without the gradings or titles with which we are familiar. A secretary may be categorised as a manager because she is doing work previously done by her manager, without ever being told that she now uses competences which previously would have put her on a managerial career path. It is probably truer to say that the scope for involvement in managerial responsibilities will increase, than that management jobs will be revived.

● ● ● The skills of the future

So is that all we need to know in order to still have a successful career? Ensure you are in a job area that is increasing in its numbers requirements and has sufficient skill requirements to ensure a good salary. Make a switch if you are not already well positioned and wait for progress to be ressumed. Unfortunately not – we still need to know more of the actual demands of those jobs. Knowing that new jobs are going to be in skill-intensive, knowledge-based occupations in service areas, when you are a qualified professional working in a service company, could result in self-delusion as to your employment value. We need to understand what companies are now meaning by skill.

> **"We need to understand what companies are now meaning by skill."**

The 1994 Skills Needs in Britain survey reports that 63 per cent of employees believe that the skills needed by an 'average' employee are increasing, and feel that their own skill levels have increased since 1986. You may well agree with these statements. You will have acquired additional job technical skills since you began your career, and the expectation to keep up to date with job-related knowledge has never been greater. These are not the only skills that employers are wanting more of. When they speak of skills they also mean:

● **Social skills** – the ability to communicate across levels with customers, other departments and across functional areas. As one manager reported in an interview with management writer Peter Drucker, 'We have more PhDs in biology and chemistry than we have janitors, and they have to learn that their customers aren't PhDs, and the people who do the work aren't'. Professionals and managers are expected to speak in language that is appropriate to the other party, and to take their cues from listening to them. Listening and giving respect is key to working effectively with different sorts of people in project teams.

● **Broadening skills** – the ability to take on a larger number of roles at the same level, taking the model of job enlargement begun in production areas into the office. Simultaneously, they are taking on jobs that previously would have involved several levels up and down the line. Management speak calls it 'empowerment', HR calls it 'job enrichment', and employees call it overload.

● **Developing core skills** – using personal skills to communicate well, to motivate themselves and others, to problem solve and to flex according to business need.

●●● New skills profile

The employee, however technically able, who does not have the ability to adapt personal behaviours and work style to the needs of different assignments, customers and colleagues, will be viewed as skills deficient. This skills profile goes well beyond the acquisition of professional qualifications, or the learning of traditional managerial skills of planning, co-ordination, resourcing and monitoring. The skills that organisations are now saying they are looking for demand a great deal more of individuals, no matter how well qualified they are. Employers are also saying that these skills are presently underdeveloped in their workforce. In the survey 53 per cent reported that there was a gap between what employees are offering and what the business now needs.

The Institute of Management reinforces this picture of a changing skill profile in its assessment of what organisations in the future will be like. In looking at how managers need to be developed to cope with the demands of the new millennium it reported that organisations will be very different.

The themes are not new, yet what this study shows is how much further we have to go before these changes are embedded in organisational practice. If you were harbouring any thoughts that the changes you have been seeing will burn themselves out, and normality will be restored, the Institute of Management's message is that your organisation has probably only just begun, although your competitors may be much further along the road.

Organisations of the future will be very different

	Very likely to happen	Largely implemented
Authoritarian management styles will be increasingly inappropriate.	50%	29%
The number of managerial layers will decrease.	49%	27%
There will be increased delegation of responsibility throughout the workforce.	43%	20%
Pay will be more directly linked to performance and/or results.	42%	17%
Most work will take place in multidisciplinary teams.	37%	19%
Managers will undertake continuous learning rather than periodic training.	34%	16%
Managers will be responsible for people who are widely dispersed, supported by the use of IT.	32%	12%

● ● ● The disappearing organisation

If organisational career paths are disappearing because of flattening structures, evidence is also growing that large organisations are becoming endangered species. In the attention given to blue chip companies, and the importance of building a career with a well-known name, we have ignored the fact that 96 per cent of all firms employ less than 20 people. To work for a large private sector organisation has never been the norm, though to look at the business press one would never suspect it. The unstartling fact is that most new firms are small firms, and while recession halted their advance in the early 1990s, their numbers are now on the rise again, with 2.8m small firms

"evidence is also growing that large organisations are becoming endangered species."

43

employing 35 per cent of those in non-public sector occupations. At the other end of the scale are the 3,000 firms with over 500 employees who currently employ one third of workers. At present the numerical differences between the two groups are not great, but the indications are that the balance will swing in favour of the petite as the 1990s proceed. It's not just that new small firms are being created. It's that while small firms are taking on staff and expect to continue to do so, according to the CBI large organisations are shedding labour and will continue to do so. The headlines of high street banks, building societies, retail organisations and privatised utilities losing staff will continue in the 90s regardless of economic recovery. At the same time, small firms in unspectacular fashion will increase their numbers. When recruitment of 10 additional staff represents a 50 per cent staff increase, it doesn't grab headlines in the same way as a supermarket group recruiting 1,000 or a utilities company shedding 10,000.

● ● ● Organisations go bonsai

For the future we will need to be looking at the business press to spot trends that could mean the creation of new opportunities rather than scanning the broadsheet papers for vacancy advertisements. We may even need help in identifying a large organisation. If growth as evidenced in the size of corporate headquarters was a sign of success for much of this century, then miniaturisation is becoming the marker of large organisations in the 90s. The decentralisation of organisations is being accompanied by a philosophical change. The question now being asked is, 'what is the maximum size we need to be in order to do this job well?' For Tom Peters the answer is a maximum size of 150, based on the size of an army unit. For Richard Branson it's even smaller with 50–60 in a business unit and a headquarters staff of 5. Parkinson's Law is dying, as organisations come to believe that individuals expand to fill the work available, rather than work expanding the organisational chart. Even more radically, there are those who talk of the

"The question now being asked is, 'what is the maximum size we need to be in order to do this job well?"

'virtual organisation' where technology will remove the need for a corporate work base, as we work from home supported by electronic communication, use 'hot desks' at regional offices when we are out on the road, or call into a local telecottage to make a video conference link with project partners in Sri Lanka and the USA. Assuming that the possibilities of technology will win out over human preference for direct social contact is dangerous. Even futurologist John Naisbitt, a staunch advocate of the 'virtual organisation', acknowledges that 'high tech needs high touch'. It is likely that organisations will continue to have a business and a social importance, but they will, according to Peter Drucker, bear a stronger resemblance to a tent, which can be pitched, and then moved on, than to a fixed monument to past success. For those looking to their future career, it is clear that such impermanent structures cannot support large numbers of conventional careerists.

● ● ● Life in the flexible organisation

There is one other feature of our future organisation which we need to take into account. Not only will it be smaller and more demanding of knowledge workers, it will also want to contract with employees in different ways. Organisations have discovered that costs can be controlled and demand fluctuations managed more effectively through having available part-time, fixed-term and job-share workers. The pattern will grow over the next decade. Until now women have been the major supply of this flexible workforce, and avoiding flexible options has been a marker of careerism. In all the organisations I have worked with male careerists have seen flexibility as a woman only policy, to be kept at arm's length. In the future it is likely that flexibility will be an expectation of full-time, professional and managerial workers through a variety of means:

● **Temporary managerial contracts** – for specific tasks, rather than an open-ended employment contract.

● **Sub-contracting** – while the 1980s saw 70 per cent of companies in one Institute of Management study sub-contracting out 'non-core' operations such as catering, cleaning, computing and personnel, the limits have not yet been defined. No business managers should assume that their work could never be sub-contracted.

● **Teleworking** – the professional who wishes to avoid commuting time is becoming the teleworker of the 90s. Managing teleworkers will become a growing challenge for the office-based manager.

● **Functional flexibility** – as restrictive practices on job demarcations collapse, it's not just operatives who are accepting flexibility. Functional specialisms only provide employment protection for as long as they are key to business objectives. A willingness to change and add functions in response to change will be an increasing feature of knowledge-based careers.

Where all this flexibility is leading us is to the **flexible firm**, an entity which was predicted early in the 1980s, but which is now establishing itself as an appropriate form for dealing with the organisation's need to combine continuity with adaptability.

● ● ● What does a flexible firm look like?

A flexible firm is one in which the organisation discriminates between the need for full-time permanent employees (permanency now being a relative term), who are central to the purposes of the business, and employees who are used according to the need for extra skill or labour. The flexible firm distinguishes between **core workers** – those whom it sees as central to its business, and where continuity is important, and **peripheral workers**, who are used on an as-needed basis. In turn peripheral workers can be divided into **just-in-time** workers and **added-value** workers.

Just-in-time workers are those who provide numerical flexibility that can be used according to patterns of demand. Contracted out services, part-time, temporary workers, term-time contracts, and job sharers all fall into this category. Often, but not always, they have been associated with the provision of relatively low skill input, where a lack of continuity or organisational knowledge is not an issue in performance requirements. In contrast, added-value workers are those brought in to do a job that the organisation does not have the skill to do or where it does not wish to create a permanent job. The contract computer programmer has been the professional leader of this trend, often looked at with envy by permanent employees who yearn for their high weekly earnings, while ignoring their insecure position and their peripheral relationship with the organisation. What began with computing has grown with the proliferation of consultancy work and the emergence of a new breed of manager brought in at times of organisational difficulty to manage the company out of crisis and then withdraw. Charles Handy was early in spotting the new organisational form, assuming that it would look something like this:

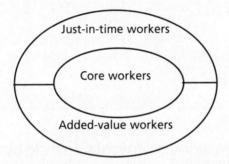

The core would be sufficiently large to exert influence on the periphery and would still offer clear career progression, even though no one employee could expect a 40-year core career. Most importantly the core would be in control of processes, because it held the organisation's memory and understood its culture.

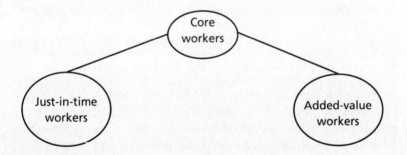

The flexible firm has come about, but its emerging form is somewhat different from that originally envisaged. Rather than the core providing the largest element, in some organisations the aim is to reduce the core to a minimum. Local authorities talk of needing no more than 100 core employees, whose role will be largely to monitor the contracts handed out to external contractors. The dramatic downsizings of TV companies has created a core now more concerned with programme commissioning and financial

"Recognising the nature of the flexible firm is key to understanding what will be required of a core career in the future."

management than programme making. Social service departments are increasingly reliant on outside agencies to provide services in the community. These are all measures of how far both the idea of a commitment to a core at the heart of an organisation and the functions of that core are now being questioned.

Recognising the nature of the flexible firm that is being created is key to understanding what will be required of a core career in the future, and for starting to consider where your skills are best placed.

Ask yourself:

● Has my organisation changed the balance between core and peripheral workers in the last five years?

● What roles and functions are currently seen as core?

● How close am I to those core areas?

● What guarantees are there that the core will not get any smaller?

● What sort of activities are now being done by peripheral workers?

● Are those activities low skilled and low pay, or are they taking on some of the most interesting assignments?

● Are people who were in the core now operating on the periphery as 'added-value' workers, or as a 'just-in-time' workforce?

● Am I seeing movement back into the core from the periphery or is it all one way?

The answers will vary, but it is likely that your organisation does not totally operate as a firm structure in which all its activities are carried out by those with permanent contracts. The balance between core and peripheral groups is likely to be in flux. There are organisations who are already discovering that the core has shrunk too far, and there are organisational costs in over reliance on a periphery, as well as managerial difficulties. Many others have only just begun the process, and it is likely to progress further. What is important for your career planning is to recognise that whether you choose a core, a peripheral or a combination career, you can take account of the expectations of each.

●●● The organisation expects

Taken together emerging trends suggest that what the organisation is expecting of its managerial and professional employees will change even from the present deal. Our employer of ten years ahead is likely to expect:

● that work will be carried out in small, largely autonomous business units, which are staffed at levels which are constantly challenged

● high performance as a prerequisite of employment

● managers who can motivate and ensure high performance from a diverse workteam which may be scattered over the globe, and many of whom will be working from home

● an acceptance of frequent changes to job content and organisational role

● a willingness to work in teams without focusing on hierarchy

● an ability to motivate people to achieve more without being able to offer them traditional performance rewards of promotion

● continuous learning and performance improvement

● managers to be responsible for teams which may comprise permanent full-time workers, part-time workers, contract workers and outsourced workers

● that job security is not assumed by any employee

● individuals will move around the organisational shape and not cling to the core.

This is a high set of expectations and, as the last chapter argued, the will of people to take them on is not assured. So what hope is there for organisations in the future? There's a risk that

"organisations are going to have to look not just at what they need to do, but also how they do it."

employees will simply dig in their heels and refuse to accept the new expectations: the final triumph of those who are intent on 'getting safe' and ' getting even'. For flexible deals even to be worth considering, from an employee's perspective, organisations are going to have to look not just at what they need to do, but also how they do it.

● ● ● Changing the way in which organisations do business

I have focused on what organisations will expect of individuals, if they are to meet the business agenda towards which the organisation is working. They are making it very clear that their demands are increasing, and will continue to do so, and that adaptability is the keynote to career survival. It's worth asking what do they need to do if they are going to get the performance expectations they see as necessary for growth? By asking this question a number of paradoxes become apparent:

● Bureaucratic systems do not sit easily with the need to innovate with speed.

● Paternalism does not sit easily with the need to foster greater individual and team initiative.

● Paternalism does not match with the removal of systems which encouraged career patronage.

● Continuous job insecurity does not create the conditions for risk taking and innovation.

● Self-development does not necessarily match with the development needs of the business; it can simply mean smart employees ensuring their external employability.

● Systems which continue to exert high control do not sit well with the need to unleash people's inner drivers for achievement.

In short, the change process cannot be all one way because

where the need is to get the most of what is in people's heads, there must be the conditions which foster contribution. In organisational culture terms, a role culture in which the value of contribution is judged by rank in the hierarchy is ill matched with the logic of maximising individual contribution. Those who have seen their work badly presented by a senior colleague, because only a senior manager can present an idea to a senior management team, will welcome this shift. The day of the team is coming, management writers regularly proclaim, and that means greater democracy in how people work together. Without greater democracy work will not be of the quality demanded. So the organisation has to loosen the ties of hierarchy, although it would be naïve to believe that even in the flattest of organisations some form of hierarchy won't assert itself. The organisation also has to show a willingness to live with anarchy, because creating the conditions for excellence means living with disorder. What are seen as the idiosyncratic ways of Silicon Valley, are looked at in admiration because of the quality of the output. The danger is that only the packaging of how they work is taken on board. The UK is now seeing the emergence of Dress Down Friday, as an acknowledgement that feeling comfortable can help people to work better, but we may miss the point. It's not that wearing jeans fosters creativity, it's that people who are creative thinkers in IT like to wear jeans. There's no reason why creativity can't come dressed in a pinstripe or even a shell suit. What's important is that people are given the conditions that encourage their creativity. For most of us, that means having greater freedom in how, when and where we work.

● ● ● What will be the career rewards of the future?

So far I have ignored the question of reward. If people are not going to get traditional career rewards, and at the same time are going to have to meet higher expectations, then we can expect that they will want other rewards. For some this will mean a greater focus on performance-related pay, although the mismatch between individual performance reward systems and team working is already evident. Others may want reward in the form of formal recognition of their contribution to a project, the opportunity to be involved in high visibility assignments, access to particular development opportunities, a sabbatical or an international job swap. The rewards we seek will be shaped by our own individual drivers, but whatever they are the message to the organisation is the same, it has to offer a range of reward systems which match with the differentiated needs of individuals.

The expectations are not all one way, if organisations are to get what they need then there are certain offers which we should expect to be in place. These could include:

● Greater freedom in how and where we work.

● Involvement in teams and projects according to our ability to contribute, not our formal rank.

● Feedback on performance, and on changing requirements of our role, so that we know when we need to make changes in how we work, if we are going to continue to be of value.

● A range of reward systems both financial and non financial, which allow us to make choices about our working lives.

● Access to flexible working options, so that we can make adjustments to our work/life balance as the conditions of our lives change.

As much as organisations are changing the way in which business is done and who does it, we need to be telling them that if there is to be a deal they have to take account of the needs of those who have the ability to contribute. The organisation that expects a 70-hour week, but won't let any of those hours be spent at home; the organisation that promotes team working and then will only give the team leader access to information; the organisation that claims to reward according to contribution, and then will not promote a high performing woman manager because she works part time, is not dealing. It is high on expectations and low on offers. What you now need to ask yourself is what you need in order to be open to a deal. Knowing what the future is likely to bring, makes you well placed to start asking, what do I need in order to have a sense of career, and what sorts of deal do I want now, and in the future?

Remember

☐ Labour market trends show that there will be an increase in the number of jobs over the next ten years and that these are most likely to be in service occupations.

☐ The labour market is segmenting into jobs which are reducing in number and skill level, and those which are increasing in number and skill level. In this segmentation managers and professionals appear as winners.

☐ The skills increase being expected of managers and professionals relates as much to the development of personal skills, as to technical competence and a broadening of the scope of their job role.

☐ Job increases are more likely in small firms than the large organisations which have created the concept of the organisational career. Large organisations are likely to continue to shed jobs.

☐ Organisations are moving towards a more flexible structure in which the workforce is divided into core and peripheral workers. For those on the core being able to add organisational value is key to their market value.

☐ The expectations that organisations have of flexibility in knowledge workers also implies a willingness in organisations to create conditions of greater autonomy and to offer a range of rewards.

*" Career resilience
cannot be built on
organisational
dependence."*

what do you expect from your career?

*'Until one is committed there is hesitancy, a chance
to draw back . . . the moment one definitely commits
oneself, then providence moves too . . . Boldness
has genius, power and magic in it, begin it now.'*
Johann Wolfgang von Goethe

We have travelled the organisational journey of the past ten
years in order to understand why from their perspective the deal
had to change, and how it will continue to change in the future.
There is no going back. However,
this organisational perspective is   **"There is no going**
only half the picture. By itself, it   **back."**
continues to place all power in
the hands of employers. For
career dealing to begin, you have to understand what you need
and want in order to have a sense of career, and how those needs
can be matched with the changing nature of work and organisations.

It is this part of the equation that has been missing in the past.
In my early years as a career counsellor, my satisfaction came
from helping people to understand their abilities and interests,
their goals and ambitions. If I succeeded, clients left with
enhanced self-confidence and a sense that they could make
things happen. 'If you can dream it, you can achieve it', was how
an American friend explained career planning to me. The idea
that we are agents in creating our own futures is a powerful and
important one, but what is missing from this view of the world is
any sense of context. It assumes that there is a stable labour
market, and that once a goal has been identified, it only needs
honed job search skills in order to gain the prize. Find the

"As the labour market has become more competitive, all those skills have become necessary, but not in themselves sufficient, for successful career planning."

person with the power to employ you. Ensure your cv focuses on your performance contribution. Practice your interview skills to deal with awkward questions, and chances of success will soar. What's wrong with such advice? Nothing – except that the prize may no longer be on offer.

As the labour market has become more competitive, all those skills have become necessary, but not in themselves sufficient, for successful career planning. If you have sent off hundreds of cvs – if you have had so many interviews that you could run your own training courses on the dos and don'ts – if you now have a personal planner bulging with names of potential contacts, and are still un or under-employed – you know that sometimes personal power is not everything. If you have always achieved above average performance appraisals, been willing to do whatever was necessary in order to get the job done, on time and on budget, and have given time to informal networking after hours, without any sign of the next promotion being visible, then you have also learnt that our future is not always in our control. We can blame ourselves for failure. This can result in even harder efforts to succeed or a decision to give up and turn away from the idea that a career is possible. An alternative is to recognise that the context is changing to an extent that it cannot give us what we have come to expect, in the way we have come to expect it. Whether you are employed or unemployed, if your career model is out of sync with reality, you are setting yourself up for a sense of personal failure.

This chapter is the starting point for beginning to look at your career, so that you can put your goals up against what is now possible, and begin assessing how a satisfactory deal can be built. Once you are clear on the sort of career that matches with your values and needs, then you can begin to assess where in the emerging model of work you will be best placed.

● ● ● Career or careering?

Chambers 20th Century Dictionary's definition of career as 'advancement in profession or occupation' does not adequately describe current experience. Often the word careering feels more accurate – a sense of rushing without knowing what is ahead, while bumping into obstacles along the way. Somewhere in the past few years the words which were once associated with career have either lost their meaning or become derided. Consider this list of word associations, which only five years ago managers gave when describing career:

● a ladder
● a path
● a race
● a roller coaster
● my life
● my security

The interweaving of a sense of self and the possibility of being able to see ahead, whether up a ladder or to the finishing line, are embedded in these associations. Ask managers now for their view of career and different word pictures are offered. These are recent comments from managers in large household name companies.

Career – what is it?

● 'I don't know any more. All I know is that what is happening at the moment isn't working.'

● 'I have no idea what career my company wants me to follow.'

● 'From a financial point of view at the present time, my future looks very bleak indeed. I have had the threat of redundancy hanging over my head for the last few years.'

● 'I need urgent reassurance that a flatter organisation still presents opportunities for career development – if that is the case.'

● 'I am now in the "lucky to have a job" category.'

● 'The word career and this company do not sit easily in the same sentence.'

The message in these statements, and hundreds like them, is one of uncertainty, of not knowing what the future means, because the past is gone and no one is telling them what lies ahead. There is both cynicism and fear in their comments. Who can feel motivated when the best that can be hoped for is surviving the next redundancy round, at which point the chances of being made redundant next time only increase. You might expect that in such an environment people would spend their days scouring vacancy advertisements, ringing up cont-acts, and looking for a way out. While some do, and especially those who have spent less time with the company, many become even more tied into their employer. Why should this be so? Why should able, ambitious people stay in an environment which daily gives them unpalatable messages? David Noer, working in the USA with those who have survived redundancies, finds individuals stay not out of loyal commitment, but because of **emotional dependence**. By dependency he means:

● Regardless of what the organisation does, they see them-selves as having no choice but to stay.

● They believe that if they can find out the right things to do, they will be safe.

● They believe that if they minimise any irritation they could cause the organisation, by never being absent, always work-ing long hours, and never doing anything that could expose them to the risk of failure, the organisation will still need them.

Dependency, in this sense, matches with the behaviours shown by the partners of those who are alcoholics, drug addicts or physical abusers. They look to find a way of minimising the risks to themselves, while also trying to increase the abuser's depend-ence on them. If this sounds a melodramatic description, then remember those managers who describe their chief career tactic as Getting Safe.

● ● ● What's your career?

What do you now say when asked about your career:

● Career – what career?

- If career means having to do what my boss does, then you can keep it.

- It's not possible to have a career and have a life

- I'm doing OK – the changes that have gone on have actually made things better for people like me, because it's got rid of the deadwood.

- Careers are only possible for those women with no family commitments

---

Or what?
- Take the temperature of your current feelings about the idea of career.
- Are you harking for the past, and still mourning its loss?
- Are you disenchanted about the present, and stuck with negative feelings, but with no sense of where to go next?
- Are you already seeing possibilities for the future that were not there before?

Are you organisationally dependent?

Then ask yourself an even more challenging question, are you organisationally dependent? By this I don't mean do you like being part of an organisation, that is an entirely different emotion, which can be highly motivating. Organisational dependence, ironically, is often strongest in those who seem to hate work the most:

- *The organisational cynic*, who can tell you how everyone always gets it wrong – but never leaves.
- *The organisational wise-guy*, who puts all the new joiners right about 'how it really is around here' – but if it's that bad, why have they stayed so long?
- *The organisational saboteur*, whose only satisfaction seems to come from showing how nothing is possible.
- *The organisational intellectual*, who can always prove that the outcome would have been different if only 'they' were smart enough to listen to those who think – but never looks for a thinking organisation.

Managers who say that their chief career driver is Getting Even, reveal themselves as organisationally dependent. Regardless of

59

"If you recognise yourself as organisationally dependent, and it's a harsh recognition to make, then career dealing cannot begin until that dependence is broken."

what the organisation does to them they will stay. They are like the woman whose response to her husband's constant infidelities was not to leave or to throw him out, but to add small doses of poison to his food. As she wreaked revenge, she simultaneously ensured he needed her to care for him.

If you recognise yourself as organisationally dependent, and it's a harsh recognition to make, then career dealing cannot begin until that dependence is broken. Wanting to stay working for your organisation because it is an enjoyable place to be, you are geographically settled, and you like your co-workers are positive emotions that can feed into career negotiations. Wanting to stay, in order to make things difficult for 'them', or because who else would want you, puts you on an unequal footing for negotiating something better. Career resilience cannot be built on organisational dependence.

● ● ● Career success – what does it mean?

Even if you are presently struggling with the idea of what a career can now be, when no one talks any more of career paths, and the succession plan has become a historical document, it's still certain that you have a model of career success. Strip away the protective armour of cynicism, and everyone holds within them a sense of what success feels like. Listen to these comments from managers, who know that further promotion is unlikely:

● *'I believe that career development is not necessarily linked to promotion. I believe that greater empowerment could mean greater job satisfaction and better use of my talents.'*

● *'I am and always have been content working for this company. I joined the organisation for long-term career prospects, stability, security . . . I will continue to work hard and loyally.'*

● *'It's not just promotion that counts, training, new skills and challenging work is more important.'*

Their words illustrate that promotion is not the only marker of a continued sense of career success. It never was, but for too long we have assumed that the word career is synonymous with advancement, and therefore those without advancement do not have a career. For two of these managers, it's knowing that they are still learning which is important to their sense of career, for the third it's an identification- with contributing to an organis ation. We have been encouraged

"We have been encouraged to see career as externally defined, when in reality it also has to be internally defined."

to see career as externally defined, when in reality it also has to be internally defined. Rely on an external assessment, and the emotional impact of taking away those external symbols can be traumatic. The organisation which takes away status different- iators little understands the emotional impact of that action for an individual who has defined himself by the increasing size of his office space, or most emotive of all, the size of the company car. To see your career as an external object, and to deny the internal experience is a self-damaging delusion. Failure to recognise your internal signals places you in a vulnerable position for future career negotiations. At its starkest a career review discussion becomes a sterile interchange:

Interviewee	I want a promotion, I'm ready for it, I deserve it.
Interviewer	You are doing a good job, but you can see that there is not a promotion position within this department.
Interviewee	If I am doing a good job, then I deserve a pro- motion. If I am not promoted, I can't be doing a good job.
Interviewer	It's got nothing to do with doing a good job, of course you are, and that's reflected in your performance-related pay, but the new structure has taken out the next level, that you would have moved into.
Interviewee	If I can't have a promotion, then how am I sup- posed to stay committed. If I can't have a new job

title, and I am doing the job that would have got me a promotion, then why can't I have the company car that went with the higher grading.

And on . . . and on . . . and on . . .

External vs internal validation

The externally focused individual needs those titles and perks in order to validate himself, because without them, in his terms, he has failed. Organisations have encouraged this sense of career, and in my experience, it is more strongly developed in men than women. The reasons are not hard to find. Given that women have not had the organisational career success of their male peers, many place less emphasis on those externals, and are driven instead by their own sense of success. It could be seen as useful rationalisation since the statistics show that women are not represented in organisations in proportion to their abilities or demographic presence. I think it is more than mere adaptive behaviour. The number of women who having made every personal sacrifice required in order to break through the 'glass ceiling', then choose to walk away from it all is increasing. They leave because they do not like the behaviours required of them as senior executives, rather than because they cannot do the job. Others report that having won the game, they decided it wasn't worth winning. Both stances are evidence that their model of career success has an internally defined dimension.

Men also have internalised career values, but the number of men who have listened to that internal voice and acted on its urgings are far fewer – and it's not just for financial reasons. Men have been encouraged to define themselves by 'what they do', because it has met with the organisation's agenda. It has encouraged greater efforts from all those competing for the same prize, the next promotion. If conventional prizes are now fewer, then it's important to start recognising what your inner voice is saying, if you are going to have a sustainable sense of career success.

Defining your career success?

Ask people what career success means to them, and they give diverse answers:

- Being able to achieve my personal goals, no matter how they might look to others.

- Making a lot of money.

- Being recognised for the skills I have.

- Being happy in my work.

- Being able to provide for my family.

- Being my own boss.

- Knowing that others will pay me for doing what I like doing.

- Knowing that what I have done has made a difference to someone's life.

- Getting to the top of an organisation – or as near as I can.

- Being recognised in the wider business community, as someone who is worth listening to.

- Knowing that because of my input something new has happened.

- Being recognised as a leader.

- Creating the life I want to lead.

- Being able to work with people who share my ideals.

The answer to the question 'what is career success?' is intensely personal. There are no right or wrong answers. The person who can only validate themselves if they sit at the top of an organisational chart has one measure, the person for whom it is knowing that they have given their best in the care of old people, and may never have been promoted in their lives, has an equally valid criterion. It is the consequences of those choices which cause us problems. Since corporate careerism attracts the financial benefits associated with success, and care work doesn't, we can be led into making correlations between career success and income. In time the relationship reverses in direction. Success comes to be defined by income, rather than being a signifier of only certain types of career success.

Regardless of how organisations structure themselves, we still need to seek a sense of career satisfaction. That is a reasonable expectation. As organisations come to define their futures in terms of 'know-how' and look to engage the skills and knowledge of professionals and managers in order to 'know beyond' their competitors, you, as one of those key personnel, have a right to start asserting your expectations of a successful career.

● ● ● Start identifying your career expectations

By answering the following questions you will be able to identify your career expectations, that is, those things which will give you a sense of career success. For each question select the box which most accurately reflects your current level of expectation and mark the matching score. For example, if promotion is a very important career expectation for you, then place a 4 in the appropriate box.

When I speak of career expectation, I do not mean what do you expect the organisation will offer you – but rather what expectations do you have for yourself? **What would make you feel a sense of career success?**

CAREER EXPECTATIONS QUESTIONNAIRE

Which of the following career expectations do you hold:

	Very Important 4	Some Importance 3	Slight Importance 2	No Importance 1
1. Promotion.	☐	☐	☐	☐
2. Control over how and when I work.	☐	☐	☐	☐
3. Being able to get a job done well through managing the efforts of others.	☐	☐	☐	☐
4. Enough leisure time to travel, relax and be myself.	☐	☐	☐	☐
5. Being the sort of executive that this company now needs for its future.	☐	☐	☐	☐
6. Being allowed to retain an in-depth area of specialist knowledge or skill.	☐	☐	☐	☐

	Very Important 4	Some Importance 3	Slight Importance 2	No Importance 1
7. Being able to contribute new ideas which will help build the future.	☐	☐	☐	☐
8. A balance between work and other areas of my life.	☐	☐	☐	☐
9. Leading a team on key organisational projects.	☐	☐	☐	☐
10. Opening up new business directions through getting new ideas off the ground.	☐	☐	☐	☐
11. Being part of an organisation.	☐	☐	☐	☐
12. Being given challenges which stretch me intellectually.	☐	☐	☐	☐
13. Being able to show that I have more to offer than my colleagues.	☐	☐	☐	☐
14. Being able to identify closely with an organisation.	☐	☐	☐	☐
15. To be recognised for my expertise.	☐	☐	☐	☐
16. Being able to influence outcomes because of having the scope to do things differently.	☐	☐	☐	☐
17. Being able to get the most out of people in order to achieve the set goal.	☐	☐	☐	☐
18. Taking the risk of getting a new business venture off the ground.	☐	☐	☐	☐
19. Getting ahead at a rate which matches my own internal timetable.	☐	☐	☐	☐

	Very Important	Some Importance	Slight Importance	No Importance
	4	3	2	1
20. Being able to put work in its place as an important, but not the only part of my life.	☐	☐	☐	☐
21. To have the status that comes with being part of a successful company.	☐	☐	☐	☐
22. To be involved in assignments which will take the business forward.	☐	☐	☐	☐
23. Having a financial stake in an enterprise where my work can influence its financial success.	☐	☐	☐	☐
24. To be put in situations which will drive me to win out over the difficulty of the task.	☐	☐	☐	☐
25. To be able to see that I am doing better than those I am in competition with.	☐	☐	☐	☐
26. Knowing that I am respected for the specialist skills that I bring.	☐	☐	☐	☐
27. Being able to work where and when I want, so long as I can deliver results.	☐	☐	☐	☐
28. Having recognition for being a generalist who can motivate others.	☐	☐	☐	☐
29. A reduced time commitment to work so that I can better manage all the other demands on my life.	☐	☐	☐	☐

	Very Important	Some Importance	Slight Importance	No Importance
	4	**3**	**2**	**1**
30. Knowing every year that I have further developed my expertise.	☐	☐	☐	☐
31. Being able to make decisions without being controlled by organisational bureaucracy.	☐	☐	☐	☐
32. The excitement of creating something new, whose success depends on me.	☐	☐	☐	☐

Work out your profile by taking your scores for each question and linking them to their expectations category.

	Questions				
	1	13	19	25	Total
Competition	☐	☐	☐	☐	☐
	2	16	27	31	
Freedom	☐	☐	☐	☐	☐
	3	9	17	28	
Management	☐	☐	☐	☐	☐
	4	8	20	29	
Life balance	☐	☐	☐	☐	☐
	5	11	14	21	
Organisation membership	☐	☐	☐	☐	☐
	6	15	26	30	
Expertise	☐	☐	☐	☐	☐
	7	12	22	24	
Learning	☐	☐	☐	☐	☐
	10	18	23	32	
Entrepreneurship	☐	☐	☐	☐	☐

What does your score mean?

The distribution of scores indicates where your current career expectations are most strongly placed. Your profile should show some differentiation between the eight categories. This is an indication that however disillusioned you may feel about the current possibilities of a career in your organisation, you still hold expectations of how your sense of career could be sustained.

Competition

An emphasis on competition shows that the idea of career as a contest in which you compete against others, and gain satisfaction from winning through to the next round, is important to you. Take away that possibility, through restructuring or a stronger focus on team working and team results and you feel dissatisfied, unless your individual contribution is recognised.

Freedom

An expectation of autonomy shows that in order for you to have a sense of career satisfaction you expect to have freedom in how, when and where you work. Your expectation is to be judged by the outcome, rather than for doing things the 'organisation way'.

Management

If you place an emphasis on management, then you have an expectation that your career is based around using generalist skills together with an ability to work with and through others, in order to deliver results. The role and status of manager is important to you.

Life balance

A focus on life balance does not indicate a low commitment to career or a reduced ability to contribute, but rather that work is one, but only one, of the roles on which you place emphasis in your life. In your career you will be looking for situations which allow you to create that balance, and will be resentful if it is denied you because of working norms or lack of flexible working practices. You will see your career as your life in total, rather than your total life as your career.

Organisation membership

If you have made organisation membership a strong expectation, then you cannot imagine a career which is not linked to the success and values of the organisation you work for.

Membership of an organisation provides you with an arena for your career, while your career is a reflection of the organisation's success.

Expertise

Expectations of the application of expertise are important to your sense of self and hence of career. A career which attempts to broaden you out of an area in which you are technically competent will be resisted, because it will erode your self-confidence.

Learning

Expectations of learning in a career are linked to the idea that one experiences oneself best through the challenge of over-coming problems and obstacles. It is through learning from difficulty, achieving a goal which may have seemed impossible at the outset, and as a result being equipped to take on an even bigger challenge, that a sense of career progression develops. A career without a constant sense of learning will feel unsatis-factory.

Entrepreneurship

If you have an expectation of entrepreneurship, then your sense of career comes from taking risks, and of seeing something grow from an idea into reality. It will be important to you that you are in the driving seat, and once the idea is embedded, your career will feel stagnated unless there is a new idea in prospect. While entrepreneurship has traditionally been associated with self-employment, you may want to apply those skills working within an organisation on new ventures. You may have little interest in growing a large enterprise, but you have a high interest in being in control of new ones.

Your profile

It is likely that no one expectation dominates your profile, but that there are a number which work together, and from which a fuller picture of yourself can be built. For example:

- Is a high score on freedom supported by a high score on entrepreneurship or learning?
- Is a high score on management supported by a high score on organisational membership?

- Is a high score on life balance supported by a high score on entrepreneurship or freedom?

What if the profile does not fit so easily?

- You are high on freedom but also high on organisational membership.
- You are high on life balance and also high on management.
- You are high on competition but low on organisational membership.

Does this mean one or other career expectation has to be ignored. I don't believe it does, and that as we explore more fully ways of working with the 'knowing beyond' organisation, you will find ways of handling these paradoxes.

● ● ● Differentiate your profile

What if your profile is flat, with little differentiation between any of the categories – you want it all, or none of it is important to you? If your results show that you want it all, then you are a career gourmand. No employment is ever likely to be able to meet this menu of need, and you are setting yourself up for disappointment – indeed it may explain your disappointment. More likely, you need to differentiate between the categories. Revisit the questions, and ask yourself, if I had to choose between any two of the categories, e.g. promotion or autonomy, entrepreneurship or life balance, which would I give up last. The things which you would give up easily show where your career expectations are strongest. They may have changed since you last thought in these terms. You may discover that the need to win out against others in an externally focused model of career has reduced in importance, while your expectation of personal autonomy has increased. You may have discovered that while it is easy to criticise your organisation, organisational membership is important to you, or that while life balance seems a rational response to reduced promotional opportunities, it is not ultimately a high preference. Alternately, you may be moving away from valuing life balance as the demands of family care diminish, and need to acknowledge that your expectations are for more visible career success. You need to be clear about your real expectations rather than your career 'shoulds' if you are going to start planning for a different future.

What if nothing in the questionnaire held importance to you? It's possible. If that is the case answering the questions may have highlighted your real expectations:

● high earnings
● having a public profile for doing something well
● working on issues that match with your personal or social values
● working with others who share your life concerns
● achieving outcomes through technology rather than people
● being able to change career direction every few years

Acknowledge those career expectations, as denying them will prevent your being in a position to start negotiating.

My career expectations are
●
●
●

There's one career expectation that was deliberately excluded from the inventory – job security. It is excluded because it cannot be an end in itself. It may result from your expertise, your managerial skills, your ability to take on challenges and overcome odds, but it cannot be a career goal. Get safe is not a career objective, because it results in behaviours which ultimately act against personal career

"Get safe is not a career objective."

security. As we have seen in the analysis of the organisation's position, security can only come from being able to contribute fully to either core or peripheral needs. The core in itself is no longer a safety burrow.

Recognising your current career expectations allows you to assess them against those of the organisation. Go back to Chapter 2 and look again at the initial expectations which you identified both for yourself and the organisation. Having spent time thinking about your career expectations, you may have found that there is more to be added to the list, or there are new insights as to the extent of the match or mismatch with what now appears to be on offer. Once you can articulate the nature of your current expectations against current realities, you are in a stronger position to start the process of matching.

Remember

☐ The erosion of the link between organisation membership and career progress is causing disenchantment with the idea that a career is still possible.

☐ The idea of career cannot be dead as long as people have a model of career success. For some people this is an external model which demands the visible evidence of job titles, pay increases and status symbols. For others it is an entirely internal model, where the only of arbiter of success is the individual. For many of us, career success includes elements of both.

☐ In order to be able to career contract, we need to be clear as to our career expectations, rather than only looking to what we expect the organisation to offer us.

☐ We each have a number of career expectations, but they can be differentiated by establishing which we must not give up, if we are to have a sense of personal success.

☐ The one career expectation which is inappropriate is job security. This is not because it is unattainable, but because as a primary goal it results in behaviours which are likely to undermine the possibility of attaining security.

" *Compare employers'*
expectations of core
and peripheral
workers and the
similarities are
greater than the
differences. **"**

let's start matching: you and the new organisation

'It would be misleading . . . to equate core workers with those who are full-time or permanent. 'Core' workers may include, for example, part-time and temporary professional staff.'
CBI

With a picture of your career expectations, you are ready to start relating them to the emerging organisational shape. Be warned, the matching process is not as simple as you might assume. Your expectations could change by the end of this chapter.

Let's start with your profile, and look at it against the three options which we identified in Chapter 3:

● core working
● peripheral working as a 'just-in-time' worker
● peripheral working as an 'added-value' worker.

The matching process seems transparent:

● Your career success is based on an expectation of working for an organisation for the rest of your life.
Conclusion – I must be a core worker.

● You know that autonomy is important to you.
Conclusion – Get me to the periphery as quickly as possible.

● Creating the life I want to live makes life-balance important to me.

> **Conclusion** – I will have to be at the periphery, and I'll accept reduced pay in order to gain time.
>
> ● I am an entrepreneur who has been thwarted by organisational rigidity.
> **Conclusion** – I'll flourish at the periphery as a self-employed contractor.
>
> ● I can only ever see myself feeling validated if I am a manager.
> **Conclusion** – I have to be in the core, or how can I have a career?

All these conclusions have a logic, but is it a logic based in history, rather than what's happening around you now? It assumes that employers' expectations of those operating in the core remains largely unchanged, and that the periphery is for unmanageable mavericks, and those with complex lives. For those who like organisational membership it makes the core seem a magnet. For those who want to break out, it makes the periphery seem a haven. Both conclusions can be wrong.

● ● ● The merging of the core and the periphery

I spent a day working with public sector managers who knew that legislation was going to reduce radically the role of their department. As a result many of them were likely to be made redundant, or at least would have to reapply for their own job against competitors. After discussing their feelings about changes to their work (largely negative), I asked them where they now expected their careers to be in five years' time. In a group of nine, eight saw themselves as core workers, the ninth defined herself as an entrepreneur. The group joked about her dissension – and were quick to point out that she would have to be self employed, while they would remain permanent employees. 'Why do you still want to be in the core, when you have spent all day telling me how difficult, frustrating and stressful it is?', I asked. 'Because job security is important', I was told. In that reply, the speakers revealed themselves as blind to the reality of what core working was going to mean. It may well be that the one entrepreneur has core membership security, because she has skills which the organisation needs to retain. She has already shown herself able to take her area of work and transform it into a business unit. In the future that organisation faces having to break old rules about how its services are delivered, and those who can bend with these changes hold key skills. Her employer will have to convince her that she is better placed staying with them than in leaving. Providing expert and loyal service, no matter how strong the commitment (and these managers were fully committed), may not hold the same currency, or offer the same security. That is a difficult truth to swallow.

Or consider the enormous growth in temporary managers. Headhunting firms have now added the placement of interim (i.e. temporary) managers into their portfolio. So fast is this market growing that official statistics suggest that 62,000 managers joined this category in 1994. The idea of a career as a peripheral managerial worker would not have existed five years ago. Then there are organisations like London Underground, Royal Mail, NatWest Bank and Powergen who, after spending large sums of money on external consultancy, often with limited results, are now establishing their own internal consultancies to work alongside any externally appointed adviser. Clients are now critically assessing the value of external experts. According to Charles Hamden-Turner of the Judge Institute of Management Studies, 'The internal consultant is more knowledgeable about the system, more aware of local particularities'. Just because the internal consultant is not on a daily consultancy rate, which puts externals under pressure to produce dynamic instant answers, the insider can look at change issues in a more culturally sensitive way. A core career as an internal consultant would have been unthinkable for most companies five years ago. It would have been derided as a move into special projects – usually the first step towards career oblivion.

Or what about the life-balancer – most likely a woman, and almost certainly expecting that her career has to be a compromise – who accepts whatever work contract is available as the price of staying in the labour market. Why shouldn't she be in the core and rewarded as such, if telecommunications mean that she can work from home, linked by pc, fax and modem, not just to the local office, but to the organisation's world-wide network of co-workers?

Spot the difference?

The truth is that divisions between the core and the periphery are becoming increasingly blurred as organisations start to redefine what they need of each. As a core worker of my organisation, I spend a considerable part of my time at home – researching, writing and dealing with clients. It makes more sense than commuting 130 miles daily on an overcrowded motorway and feeling my energy level drop as the week progresses. As long as I can be reached and can respond to client needs, it doesn't matter where I input my work. Clients often don't know I am working at home. I can call into my voice mailbox to pick up phone messages, and can connect through my pc into e-mail, so I am constantly in touch with new workplace information. I am frequently a core worker at a distance. What is important, in order to justify my continued place in the core, is that the quality of my output meets expectations, and that the output is critical enough in supporting the organisation's business goals to justify my continued employment.

At the same time I work alongside peripheral workers who can spend more time in the workplace than I do. They are delivering programmes to managers in a residential centre, which can demand their 24 hour presence for five-day periods. They deliver specialisms that are not available in the core, but for which the organisation does not have sufficient demand to justify offering full-time contracts. In order that their skills are utilised and valued, they consciously develop a strong relationship with the core. They spend time understanding how the business operates, sell work for the organisation, network with core employees, and feed in information which they acquire because of having a wider frame of reference. The client may have no idea that the contract worker is not a full-time employee. They come along to development events, social occasions and are given business information. The periphery and the core are strongly interdependent, and the success of the organisation is understood to depend on both. This is a very different view of periphery working from that I experienced some years ago when working alongside contract programmers. They were present from 9–5 pm, but not a moment longer unless overtime was on offer. They had little interaction with other contractors, were often resented by permanent employees who were envious of their daily rate, and ensured that no one knew too much about what they did, in case a core worker was able to take the work away from them. Financially it was an attractive deal but, as one contractor told me, 'I spent three years with ——————— and during the whole time I learnt nothing about the business, I was never included in social events, and I received no training.' The company kept its headcount down, a key issue in the growth of peripheral working, but it's doubtful if it got full value from that specialist, or was able to transfer the learning into the core.

> **"Positioning your career against the flexible firm is a more complex process than it appears at the outset."**

Positioning your career against the flexible firm is a more complex process than it appears at the outset. While the shrinking core and the expanding perimeter are self-evident, it seems that the requirements of each are not easily distinguished. Reducing layers has been done in the name of shortening the chain of command so that decisions are taken more swiftly. While organisations have made people redundant, they have often at the same time been recruiting people whom they see as having the skills required for the future. The shift from hierarchy to team working is intended to produce new and better products and services. The core has to be a source of innovation, which works in partnership with the periphery or it will be developing a dangerous dependency on contractors whose commitment can never be assumed.

●●● We are all contingent workers

Instead of seeing the core vs periphery argument as one of permanent vs temporary employees, according to William Bridges, we need to acknowledge both as 'contingency workers'. Wherever you sit within the organisation, you are only there for as long as your contribution meets productivity needs. The expectations of each group may not be not so different.

What is expected of a core worker?

If we accept the messages being given in the management press, being a core worker in the future will demand:

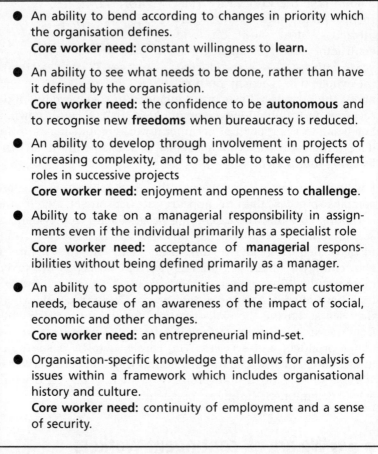

- An ability to bend according to changes in priority which the organisation defines.
  Core worker need: constant willingness to **learn.**

- An ability to see what needs to be done, rather than have it defined by the organisation.
  Core worker need: the confidence to be **autonomous** and to recognise new **freedoms** when bureaucracy is reduced.

- An ability to develop through involvement in projects of increasing complexity, and to be able to take on different roles in successive projects
  Core worker need: enjoyment and openness to **challenge.**

- Ability to take on a managerial responsibility in assignments even if the individual primarily has a specialist role
  Core worker need: acceptance of **managerial** responsibilities without being defined primarily as a manager.

- An ability to spot opportunities and pre-empt customer needs, because of an awareness of the impact of social, economic and other changes.
  Core worker need: an entrepreneurial mind-set.

- Organisation-specific knowledge that allows for analysis of issues within a framework which includes organisational history and culture.
  Core worker need: continuity of employment and a sense of security.

What is expected of an added-value peripheral worker?

Compare the expectations of core and peripheral workers, and the similarities are greater than the differences:

- To be able to offer a depth of expertise that is not readily available in the core.
  Added-value worker need: technical expertise and a frame of reference drawn from **knowledge of many organisations**.

- To be able to understand the organisation and how it operates, and to bring new solutions.
  Added-value worker need: a quick response to learning **challenges** and an **involvement with the organisation**.

- An ability professionally to manage assignments and customer relationships.
  Added-value worker need: project management skills.

- Availability when needed.
  Added-value worker need: ability to work excessively hard at times in order to meet the customer's agenda, and in order to buy 'freedom time'.

- To acquire learning, knowledge and skills at a faster rate than the organisation.
  Added-value worker need: to be constantly **learning**, and greedy for more learning.

Looked at in this way there is more that binds the core and peripheral workers than separates them. For both groups there is an expectation that they are constantly learning, and that they can apply that learning to more demanding assignments. For both there is a need to be able to manage even if the prime focus of their contribution is technical, and for both management includes the working relationship between the core and the periphery. What separates them from the organisation's perspective is that one can add value because it knows the organisation well, understands its customers, and can develop knowledge and skills which are so specific to the organisation that it will not want to lose them. While the other is of value specifically because it can help the organisation to look at itself differently. It can ask difficult questions, it can challenge the assertion that things can't be done, by showing how it has elsewhere. It can help them change, because he or she has helped others change in the same way, and so has the knowledge and confidence to embrace rather than resist change.

● ● ● But it's not like that here!

As I write these sentences, I can hear howls of protest 'But it's not like that here!'

Autonomy – what autonomy? The main use of IT is to reduce the autonomy we once had.

Projects – we've tried those, it just meant lots of wasted time, with no visible output. If you want to get through your work, keep away from being involved in projects.

Learning – if we learn it's only by accident, and the only people who talk about a 'learning organisation' are in HR.

Entrepreneurship – well that soon gets driven out of anyone who has any smart ideas.

You are right. It probably isn't like that where you are, and it's important to recognise this. It's essential not to buy automatically into a future which is too often based on the world of West Coast America. It's stimulating to hear that at Microsoft there are no regular hours (which can mean 24-hour working in order to deliver the output); that individuals are accountable to a project team, not an individual manager; that everyone collaborates because they always have to do more than any one individual could achieve; and that careers are built through project reputation. The problem is it doesn't explain how things are for you. Microsoft has had less than twenty years to establish its culture and systems, your organisation may have had two hundred. Microsoft's *raison d'être* is developing the potential of technology. Is that your organisation's reason for being? It attracts people of high ability who demand freedom as part of their skills exchange. Is that what people seek as a fair exchange for their abilities in your workplace? It is American! What's more it is not even typical of how American organisations operate, which is why it is so attractive to writers on organisations.

● ● ● What's in the core of your organisation?

You are right to challenge any global assertions of what will be required of core workers, but it's also certain that there will have been some changes. Instead, ask yourself what are the requirements of core workers in your organisation right now? Before answering, dump your initial negative thoughts:

- compliance
- brown nosing
- lack of criticism
- etc. etc.

Focus instead on what you know about the business environment in which you are operating.

In order to meet the demands being made on it, your organisation needs core workers who can:

●
●
●
●

I can't know what your list looks like. It will vary, depending on whether you are in the public, private or voluntary sector. It will be different if you are answering as a worker in an insurance company, manufacturing plant or fast food operation. It will depend on what stage your organisation has reached in the process of shedding its core. In 1994 the Institute of Personnel Development found that while 40 per cent of companies still had 90 per cent core workers, there are nearly 20 per cent with less than 50 per cent of its workers in the core, and a small percentage where only one in ten is a permanent full-time employee. The smaller the core, the more strategic will be the expectations of those left behind, and the greater the responsibility they hold for ensuring the future.

The corollary to this is that organisations differ in how peripheral workers are used. The organisation for whom 90 per cent of employers are contractors has very different expectations than the organisation where only the catering operation is outsourced. Does it seem to you that your peripheral workers are exploited, expendable labour with no sense of connection to the heart of the business? Or are those on the periphery seen as essential partners, where there is mutual self-interest in building an ongoing relationship. When you look at how peripheral workers are being used in your present environment, does it hold any appeal?

● ● ● The important differences

Recognising differences in how each group is used can help you clarify where you want to be, but the true differentiator lies in individual differences. Ask anyone who has changed from being a core to a peripheral worker, and the pay-offs which they sought become clear. Here are four answers from former core workers who have recently become self-employed:

'I just love knowing that if I want to I can take a day off to have a picnic with a friend.'

'Being able to be involved in my youngest child's upbringing, in a way I never did when I was building an organisational career, is an enormous bonus for me as a man.'

'To be able to say, "No, I don't do that type of work anymore", gives me an enormous buzz. Knowing that I can define what I do is the biggest perk of all.'

'Even though much of my work is done for my former employer, it's a completely different feeling, coming in as an associate – I feel different, and I look at the organisation differently.'

Each of them is articulating the pay-offs they sought in making the switch. For those who are happy at the edge, these are perks which can outweigh a drop in earnings. For some peripheral workers, seeing oneself as an entrepreneur is an added bonus. Defining how large an income you want for the next year, and being willing to do whatever is necessary in order to achieve it can be enormously exciting. It can provide another arena for the sense of competition which is necessary for their sense of self-worth. For others, self-employment was not necessarily sought, and entrepreneurship may be the least of their career expectations. In January 1994, the National Westminster Bank's Small Business Unit reported that 57 per cent of those starting up businesses gave a white collar job as their previous occupation, and that redundancy, rather than a desire to be one's own boss was a prime motive. The reluctant entrepreneur is a new professional career reality, where the pay-offs of imposed change only become apparent over time.

● ● ● Core contributors

What of our core workers? For them the only expectations which may distinguish them from their former colleagues is the hope of further internal competition. Within the core, there will be those whose prime motive is conventional careerism – for whom a career without an organisational position is no career. Regardless of what futurologists predict, there will still be a need for people who can take strategic business decisions, head up business units, and lead organisations. Organisations will still provide such opportunities, so the aim is then to define what succeeding will require in the future. What it requires at present is a willingness to forego life balance and it is this, more than any other expectation, which divides our two groups. The added-value workers may complain that they work longer hours than they ever did as employees, but they know that it is they who are driving that decision, and that they have the choice of controlling their workload. For our core worker, unless family-friendly policies become a larger feature of the work environment, it can be expected that they must forego balance. In the changing shape of work, any sense of responsibility which employers have felt for supporting care needs could be pushed out as a responsibility for individuals to deal with, through opting for peripheral working. Unless, that is, demanding such policies becomes part of the core employees' deal.

● ● ● What about our just-in-time worker?

With all the attention given to added-value workers, it is easy to forget that the periphery also contains many whose contribution meets another expectation.

> **Expectations of just-in-time workers:** to be available as a resource when it meets the organisation's need.
> **Just-in-time worker need:** to have a skill that can be applied quickly and readily, without requiring an in-depth knowledge of an organisation, or training.

The summers that I spent as a chocolate biscuit packer, the Christmas holidays spent as a postal sorter and the Saturday job selling hardware in a local Coop were all peripheral working – though no one would have called it such. Organisations have always used the less skilled as temporary workers – whether daily hired dockers, seasonal hamper packers or student workers. The difference is that such jobs now increasingly provide the sole means of employment for individuals who would wish it otherwise. Amin Rajan's analysis (in Chapter 3) of where jobs will be in the future showed that many new jobs with a declining skill requirement will fall into this category. So does it have any place in the career future of professionals and managers? You might think not, but it can offer a career option for those who want their working lives to be a mosaic, who want to put together their own career picture made up of a range of activities which meet particular needs. The same individual may combine a low skill activity for which there is a predictable demand and a guaranteed income, alongside high skill level work, where demand is more unpredictable.

For most knowledge workers there will be a desire to define skills that can be used to distance themselves from a just-in-time group, because they recognise the vulnerability to which it exposes them. In the rest of the book, therefore, I will focus on developing a career as an added-value worker, because I believe that not to do so diminishes the contribution which people are capable of giving. It is important, however, not to ignore the opportunities that just-in-time peripheral working can offer for shaping the life you want to lead. Just-in-time can be a transition support during a time of career change, or when you are building the value of your key skills. It has long been acknowledged as such by artists and actors, but there's no reason why it should not play a more accepted part in supporting the multiple careers that most of us will follow. The key differentiators between our three groups are:

Core working Seeks to create personal security through a willingness to accept and adapt to changing organis-ational needs, because of a desire for continued organis-ational membership.

Just-in-time working A willingness to accept temporary employment in order to meet life-style needs. Security comes from being able to control and manage different role demands.

Added-value workers Seeks to ensure personal security through selling the value of their skills to clients. Toler-ates insecurity in order to gain freedom and autonomy in how they work.

●●● So where are you?

I have argued that there is much that links core and peripheral workers, in terms of the organisation's expectations of both groups, but that for individuals there are differences in where they will feel most fulfilled. Now it's time to ask yourself:

● Do you know what shape your organisation is moving towards?

● Do your expectations and your understanding of the organisation's expectations suggest that you can continue to have a core career?

● Do your expectations and the organisation's expectations suggest that the periphery is going to be a natural place for you to be?

● Can your expectations only be met through being part of an organisation?

● Can your expectations only be met through breaking free from an organisation?

● Can your expectations only be met within the organisation if you make changes to how you work, and how you view career?

● Can your expectations only be met as an added-value worker, if you ensure you develop before moving out from the core?

It's time to own up as to how you want your next career stage to be.

I want my next career stage to be:

My career expectations can best be fulfilled within my present organisation because:

Or:
My career expectations can best be fulfilled within another organisation because:

> *Or:*
> **I think I would gain more career satisfaction as an added-value peripheral worker because:**

If only by being part of a company can you validate your career, that's fine, and future chapters will make clear what will be required, and what you can ask for in return. If life outside the organisation has appeal because of the freedoms it could offer, then that's fine also, but you need to plan in order for it to be a successful switch. From now on your personal portfolio needs to be filling up. If it's clear that staying in the core isn't an option over the medium term, that gives you the opportunity to use remaining organisational time to prepare you for what's next. If the rug is about to be pulled away, then you'll need to use the next chapters to hone your sense of what you have to offer.

Development the key to any satisfactory deal

There's no single deal that is going to meet the needs of all employees. The need for more individualised dealings with employees has to be part of future career management, but there's one element that has to be part of any deal that is put in place, and that is development. Not self-development, as in, 'We no longer have a training budget so everyone must develop themselves', or 'Since there's no career route any more it's up to individuals to look after themselves', but development as an exchange for what you offer. Remember that if you give time to an organisation, you risk reducing your external employability, unless you are constantly being developed in ways that ensure you have a wider market value. When managers with twenty years' experience tell me they are unemployable elsewhere, they are often right, not because they are incompetent, but because in the last twenty years they may not have developed beyond meeting the demands of their existing job. In those twenty years they have often failed to look at the world outside corporate headquarters. They may never have been on an external course, had a discussion to draw up a personal development plan, or given a conscious thought to learning. They have learnt a lot, but would find difficulty articulating it in ways that would highlight its transferability to other organisations.

Similarly, if you move to the periphery and fail to invest constantly in your own development, then the value of your offerings diminishes year by year. If you are a just-in-time worker and the organisation never offers you any training, then they are failing to get the most out of you, and you may eventually undermine their efforts. When peripheral workers are often representing the organisation to its customers, an organisation which ignores this group is only damaging itself. Wherever you see your career moving, one expectation which you must hold of yourself is:

DEVELOPMENT DEVELOPMENT DEVELOPMENT

Getting the deal you want now, and planning for changing the deal will be the theme for part two of this book. You know what's happening from the organisation's perspective, you know what's important to you, now you can start moving forward.

Remember

☐ The organisational expectations of core and peripheral workers are becoming less distinct. Those who are most attracted to the core may not have the skills which are sought by the core. You need to be open-eyed about what is required of core working.

☐ Being a peripheral worker is primarily distinguished by the freedom which it offers from organisational controls, although it may be equally or more demanding of your time.

☐ Gaining a life style of mixed roles is most easily achieved as a just-in-time worker, but the reduced skill expectations and view of these employees as a 'reserve army of labour' makes them a vulnerable resource.

☐ Wherever you choose to fulfil your career, you need to place development as a high expectation both on your employer, and on yourself. Without a constant focus on development your career currency will daily diminish.

"It's better to leave the cast of a soap opera with an option of returning, than to so enrage the show's producers that they kill you off.**"**

the bridge

'Never look back in anger, nor forward with fear, but around you in anticipation.'
Anonymous

Something may have struck you in reading this far – I haven't defined what a career will be in the future. I have spoken about what a career was – secure, predictable, an object that could be measured in terms of how far up a ladder an individual had climbed, set against an age norm decided by the sector. Get your first promotion as a retail manager at 40, and you are clearly 'off track'. Get your first promotion from MP to Junior Minister at 40, and you are a 'fast tracker'. Continuing to use that measure in the 1990s ensures there is a mass sense of career failure. I have also looked at what careers are at the moment, in terms of a subjective sense of disappointment, powerlessness and betrayal that mark the careers of many knowledge workers. We have looked at what you need in order to have a subjective sense of career well-being, and how that matches with the shape that your organisation is taking on. But the question of what will a career be like still sits hanging in the air.

Robin Linnecar of Career Consultants KPMG talks of careers now being like crazy paving: 'You have to lay a lot of ground work to get it right, and nothing quite fits. There is an overall direction, but it's unknown how you are going to make it work.' For him the path has been broken up, and it's up to you to lay a new one. Trying to put the pieces together can produce something which is visually inelegant, and feels uneven under-foot. Others speak of it as a career tree. Rather than a career route visible ahead, there is a tree which can branch out in all directions, and requires strong roots spread wide in order to get adequate sustenance. William Bridges talks of careers of the future being constructed like a cable woven from multiple strands, so that if any one strand frays the cable still retains its strength. Charles Handy introduced us to the idea of seeing a career as a personal portfolio, which holds our personal investments and displays our achievements to prospective clients. All these interpretations are based on a view of the individual taking control. The definition I believe describes careers in the future accepts those elements, but brings together you and your employer. For the rest of this book the view of career from which the arguments will develop is this:

> **Your career will be a series of negotiations of the psychological contract between you and your employer.**

What does this mean? It lacks the immediate appeal of describing a career in metaphor terms. It doesn't have the punch of speaking, as many consultants do, of the career of the future being the marketing of 'Me Ltd'. Put in a more direct way, from now on:

> **Your career is going to be a series of deals that seek to match your interests and those of an employer.**

The distinction which I am making is that career self-management does not have to mean pure self-interest, with an organisation regarded as something to exploit, as an arena for self-advancement before abandonment, on the premise that it's better to get them before they get you. Instead an organisation can be a theatre for a series of careers, each based on a different type of deal. A deal is possible, as long as each side is able to negotiate from a basis of looking to match expectations and offers. For evidence that this is possible look at the career of Julie Allan.

● ● ● Julie Allan: a new deals career manager

Julie Allan has had a varied working life, but a continuing theme has been her relationship with *Radio Times*. She originally joined as a listings sub-editor, a remorseless weekly schedule, where speed and 100 per cent accuracy are vital. After a year she was ready for more so she negotiated a three-month attachment to the Features department, where she was able to get involved in the sub-editing of features, and liaise with programme producers, designers and commissioning editors. When a full-time position came up she applied and was rejected, because she was told the appointment board was impressed by the calibre of external candidates. Her attachment over, conventional career-ism, for a professional in their 20s would argue get out, your career is going nowhere. Julie shared that sense, but instead of leaving she negotiated another short-term attachment to Features, and when a permanent job came up some months later she was appointed.

The new position gave her the opportunity not only to sub-edit the children's pages but also to write. Her career was now seemingly back on a conventional track of progression, but the internal environment of *Radio Times* was changing. The BBC had lost its monopoly on the right to print its weekly listings, which meant increased competition for the TV magazine market, and the appointment of a new editor. For Julie there was also a change process underway. She had been developing her interest in theatre, through running drama workshops for children, and was also keenly interested in health and exercise. The two came together in the idea of training as an exercise teacher and teaching classes to children. So far these had been leisure interests, but when the new editor joined she knew he would be looking to make changes. She decided to initiate a negotiation, based on mutual interest. He wanted greater control of journalists, which would allow for a quicker response to stories than was possible when relying on freelancers. She wanted a three-day week which would allow her to develop her other interests. He wanted someone who knew the way things were done at the BBC and could make the systems work. She knew the systems. The result was the creation of an entirely new post, that of staff writer. She became a freelance writer based in the organisation, while also acting as a consultant to an exercise company for the under fives, and running corporate fitness classes for adults. After a year, she was ready for change. The writing was not offering enough diversity so she took time off to travel in the USA, though still doing some freelance work for *Radio Times* en route.

On her return she negotiated a freelance contract with a publishing house part owned by the BBC. There she worked as

Chief Sub-Editor on a company magazine, while continuing her freelance writing. She also became involved in special projects for *Radio Times*: investigating possible offshoot magazines from programmes and putting together dummy issues. One can now see this as a career firmly at the periphery, except that she then negotiated to move back into the core as Chief Features Sub-Editor on *Radio Times*. She deliberately chose to go into a full-time middle management post. Why? Again the reason lay in changes in her. By this time she was involved in Gestalt, a method of psychotherapy based on the need to integrate thoughts, feelings and spirit in order to function effectively. The connection between the need for an integrated individual system, and for that same integration within organisations was obvious to her. She saw much dysfunctionality in how organisations worked, and she was interested in how she could impact on that as a manager (and how it might impact on her). A conscious desire for the experience of management responsibility and how she could influence a department's effectiveness led her to reverse the direction of her career moves.

She spent a year in the post, before she decided that she wanted to learn more. She is now completing a MSc in Occupational Psychology at Nottingham University, and continuing her training in gestalt. Does this mean the end of any further connection with *Radio Times*? Julie does not reject the possibility of returning. She enjoys the 'texture of organisations', the fact they are complex open systems (like herself) and can imagine herself working with the BBC in the future, but on an entirely different basis. Her next career negotiation could be with BBC magazines or BBC Worldwide on the basis of helping look at people issues at a strategic level. She won't be looking for a full-time job, but she would enjoy being part of a multi-disciplinary team working on the business/people link.

What can we take from Julie Allan's story? All her decisions have been based on recognising changes in herself, i.e. her need for a new psychological contract. She has recognised when what she is wanting is changing, but also when what she can offer is developing. At the same time, she has looked to match her needs with the changes in the business environment. Key to it all has been her ability to sustain strong relationships with colleagues and especially her editors. Making it work has depended on keeping communication going with the organisation, so that she can re-enter. It's a very different model of career management than that which has seen leaving an organisation as the only response to career disappointment. There are two further themes which mark each negotiation. Each has been based on a spiralling model of career. As she acquires new skills, both inside and outside work, she looks to use them as propulsion for opening up the next career loop. There is an internal time clock which makes her take stock of herself every eighteen months and to seek a new spin on her working life. When she is learning and enthused, she has vast amounts of energy which enable her to achieve a great deal. When that learning process slows and, in her words, she 'is not being fed by what I am doing', her energy dissipates. She monitors that process so that she can recognise the time for change. The other theme and the core within the spiral is her desire for communication. From her time as a student when she worked on student radio, to a period working in PR, through drama workshops, writing, teaching and therapy there is a commitment to communicating as the element which steadies the spiral. Recognising the centrality of communication and learning in shaping her career decisions makes it possible for her to see herself as having a career, when to others 'stepping outside a conventional career, and being your own entrepreneur makes you seem strange'.

● ● ● Isn't it time we got adult with each other?

Julie Allan's career is further marked by an ability to deal with the organisation as an adult. She is clear about what she needs and also about what the organisation needs, and she looks to make the connection. She also accepts that the organisation may not always want her, and that it is not responsible for her. Dealing on an adult-to-adult basis is unlike many traditional careers dealings. If we look at careers from the perspective of transactional analysis we find that interactions have too often been parent to child.

The organisation as parent has bestowed career gifts as a reward for effort. This has encouraged compliance in the employee child, and prevented them seeking their own independence – like the parent who offers an allowance and then cannot understand why their offspring can't get their life sorted out and keeps

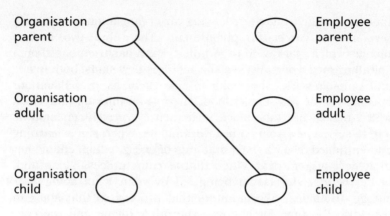

coming back for more. Or it has seemed a punishing parent who withholds career gifts, resulting in silent resentment, vocal rebellion or increased efforts to please. If an employer seeks to stand as parent it may also find itself interacting with the parent in the employee; the one who also seeks to control: 'If you don't give me that job/salary increase/bonus, I will make life very difficult for you.' Can an organisation be childlike? Of course. The small acts of meanness enacted on those who dare to leave have often come from a childlike sense of having been abandoned. Organisations (usually in the person of a line manager) and individuals are capable of being both childlike and parental in how they seek to manage careers. Career dealing is only possible, however, on the basis of treating each other as adults:

"Career dealing requires an assertive adult mind set."

● Look each other in the eye and listen to what the other is saying.

● Accept that change is inevitable (for both parties) and part of development.

● Be willing to look for a solution that is workable for both interests.

● Do not see the other as responsible for our fate.

Career dealing requires an assertive adult mind set, which does not look to blame the other and does not see itself as a martyr.

It is the interaction of the individual and the organisation which separates it from 'Meism'. 'Meism' can simply be the child acting out their rage at no longer being given the ball to play with, while simultaneously refusing to look the parent in the eye.

Ask yourself where your career negotiations have been based:

- How often have you seen your employer as a career parent who has gifts to offer and withhold, evoking in you a response that you have to please, manipulate or just accept whatever they say?
- How often has career disappointment engaged your career child – a desire to get your own back, leave home in a rage, or increase your compliance in order to win favour again?
- Have you used your career parent to try and outcoerce them?
- How often have you negotiated your career from the sense of being an adult negotiating with an adult, with equal rights on both sides?

Dealing with each other as adults is the key to your career resilience, because it puts back in your hands a sense of control. It also makes demands of you as an individual responsible for driving your career and your career choices.

● ● ● Why should organisations deal with you? - the business case

I can still hear the question 'why should organisations bother?' When the power is all in their hands surely it makes sense for them to want to hang on to being career parent. In good times they can use it to offer benevolence and in difficult times it allows them to control. This is what a colleague told me when he wandered into my office and said, 'This career stuff is fine for individuals, but organisations only care about the bottom line. They don't care about careers.' In one sense he's right. They don't care about our career in the way that we do as individuals, but they do care about motivating individuals to deliver good performance, which is why careers have always been offered.

If, like him, you have not been convinced by my previous arguments that, in order to innovate, organisations have to create the conditions which encourage people's innovation, then let me add some further evidence. This time from Geoffrey Lane, winner of the FT/MCA management essay award in 1995. He talks of the need to create a 'virtuous organisation', one which seeks to add value to itself in order to sustain its longevity. Adding that value means building the value of what he calls the 'relationship holders'. As an employee you are one of the relationship holders on whom its future depends. Building those relationships relies on recognising that loyalty is based on 'mutual self-interest, constantly reaffirmed over time'. What is more it also relies on recognising that 'Organisations are no different from people. Both desire to live long and well, doing some good along the way. They have the same basic needs for security, safety and a sense of belonging. They also desire to fulfil their potential, seeking growth, admiration from peers and justifiable self-respect.' It is in an organisation's self-interest to deal well with those on whom their future depends, but this dealing has to be on the basis of adult relationships. It means telling employees the truth and not pretending that there is a traditional career future, if there is not. It means giving people feedback that is direct. It means laying out the future and letting people make their choices as to how they can work within those futures. As Geoffrey Lane comments, 'The virtuous organisation is not a soft place to be. If anything it is tougher than many because it deals in realities, honestly and openly.' Lane's argument is all the more convincing because he is not an academic, but a senior manager with a major banking group: a sector which has seen radical changes in its career offerings to staff and where resistance has been vocal.

If you want more evidence that there is a rational beyond soft humanism in the idea of career dealing, then look to James Champy. He is heralded as the father of business process re-engineering; the management movement which has driven much recent downsizing, in the name of busting bureaucracy and rationalising the delivery of fragmented services. In his latest book, he acknowledges that there is now a need to 'get back to developing places where we have a substantive new covenant with people, and where we have the kind of person we want, and where respect for the individual is restored'. He doesn't back off from arguing that the nature of managerial work has to change since re-engineering demands pushing accountabilities away from managers, taking away hierarchy with it. However, he is now acknowledging that employer expectations cannot change, without also addressing the offers which have to be put in place to compensate for that shift. James Champy is recognising the need to deal with the softer side of management, because it makes business sense.

It's an argument reinforced by Professor Jeffrey Pfeffer of Stanford University Graduate School. He cites evidence that the distinguishing feature of the top five performing companies in the USA between 1972 and 1992 was not their technology, patents or strategy, but their approach to managing their work-force. 'You can't provide a great customer service if your employees are miserable,' he says. Competitive advantage comes from people, not from investing in computer technology. There is a growing business case that it's worth the effort of listening to and dealing with knowledge worker employees, because of the potential business downside of not doing so. It's also a natural extension of the changing relationship between organisations, their suppliers, customers and competitors. Organisations now talk of being in partnership with suppliers, where once the power differential was all too clear. They want to build strategic alliances with competitors in order to enter new markets, rather than dismissing them as inadequate enemies. They recognise the need to listen and work with customers rather than deciding what is best for them. If the business future is being premised on building adult relationships, why not your career future?

Hoskyns – a company committed to increasing its employees' market value

It's this argument which has inspired computer services giant Hoskyns now to talk openly of building employees' market value. What may seem like selfless stupidity in a sector where skills are still in short supply and where employee loyalty has been notoriously contingent on pay, has a clear logic, according to HR Director Carolyn Nimmy. The business has moved over time from a primary focus on technology, to delivering clearly defined services and products to their customers. This is no longer enough. Customers are expecting that as suppliers they should also understand their business, and help them solve business problems. Hoskyns now defines itself as helping customers to run their businesses better with IT. Technical expertise is not sufficient. For the individual to achieve a high customer utilisation rate, they need also to be developing their business skills. Increasing market value is primarily about ensuring staff are valued by customers. They expect that the IT professionals who are sent to them are skilled and marketable. If they are not they will look elsewhere. For Hoskyns it is a necessary investment, and if the investment is not returned by the individual's continuous employment on assignment, it will be quickly spotted and the problem addressed.

As part of the commitment to increasing market value, consultants complete monthly quality reports, not just on their technical and commercial input, but on their personal assessment of quality, through being asked to assess whether the work they are doing is helping them achieve their personal targets. This is not blind idealism; it is a clear-sighted assessment that if people are working towards personal goals their commitment to high service delivery will be greater. There is no evidence that giving individual development such a high focus has increased exiting – but there is clear evidence of an adult-to-adult approach to career dealing.

● ● ● The key processes for career dealing

The rest of this book is devoted to helping you career deal more effectively, so from now on you may want to select which of the chapters you read. If you know that your career can only be successful for you if you are a core member, then Chapters 7 and 8 will help you recognise the deal that is being sought by the organisation, and how you can work with that. If peripheral working is your aim then Chapter 9 will help you build your value so that you can operate successfully and escape exploitation. If you know that you would like to change but are unsure what you want and how you could work towards it, then Chapters 10 and 11 ask you to consider your own skills in self-monitoring and coping with transitions. Building our inner reserves to live with the career uncertainties that are likely to be a permanent feature of working lives is the theme of Chapter 12. Enhancing your negotiation skills is the focus of Chapter 13. For everyone, the practical implications of the new deals cannot be ignored, so for help in financial dealing look at Chapter 14. We'll meet up together at Chapter 15, where we'll take stock of where we've reached and the lessons learnt.

Before you leap forward, I want to lay down the key processes that will shape whichever deal you choose, because they will underpin each of the chapters. In order to be able to career deal you are going to need to pay attention to:

Information

You are going to be a reconnaissance agent, constantly collecting information on what's happening around you. You are going to be looking both inside and outside the organisation to pick up trends, to notice what is and what is not being done. You will use the official and the unofficial information systems in order to be in control of information and its implications for you. You will need to start looking at information from the position of what do these changes offer for my career options, rather than what does this mean for the job I hold.

You are also going to be gathering information on yourself. What do you know about the value of your skills, your experience, and their criticality to the organisation's future? What development do you need in order to be adding value?

At the same time you need to be giving the organisation information. How much do they know about you? Do they know where your developing interests are? Do they know or recognise the potential of skills you may have used elsewhere? Do they know what your career expectations are? Just because they are bad at asking for information, it doesn't mean you shouldn't offer it.

Negotiation

It hardly needs saying that in order to create a new career deal you are going to have to negotiate, but how well developed are your negotiating skills? If you have never seen your career as one of negotiation, then there are some skills to be learnt. If your career has been built on using your expert power or scarcity value, then you may never have had to negotiate, you may have been able to bludgeon your way through to your own ends. In that case you too need to learn to negotiate through recognising the other's position. In negotiation terms we are looking to create a win-win for each party.

Monitoring

Knowing when the deal needs to change from the organisation's side or should change from your side means paying closer attention to monitoring. You must monitor the environment, but also monitor changes in you. You need to be taking stock of changes in your life, the roles you have, your expectations of yourself, the demands on you, in order to recognise when it's time to start changing the deal. No matter how attractive the deal may look to others, if it's no longer satisfying you, then it's time to start finding out why.

Renegotiation or exit

'For everything there is a season, and a time for every purpose under heaven.' This means there will come a time when you or the organisation will want to renegotiate. Those are our career transition points, when we have a choice of negotiating with a view to our career future, or of capitulating with a fatalistic sense that our career is now over. Renegotiation as a career dealer will call on all of the above processes. Allowing for renegotiation, rather than seeing exit as the only option, can open up opportunities that may not be realisable in negotiations elsewhere. Or perhaps the preferred option will be to negotiate an exit that leaves you options for returning – after all it's better to leave the cast of a soap opera with an option of returning, than to so enrage the show's producers that they kill you off.

Remember

☐ Careers can be viewed as objects to be measured against, or as subjective feelings of well being or dissatisfaction. Career dealing, however, is based on a model of careers as successive negotiations of the psychological contract that exists between ourselves and our employer. This is true whether we are full-time or part-time, permanent or temporary workers.

☐ Seeing our career as a succession of negotiations then defines career success as obtaining a deal which matches with our needs at any point in time, and matches with the needs of an employer. It also allows for us having careers that flex in many directions, without judgements being made as to what is a 'good career'.

☐ Career dealing is only possible from a position that views individuals as capable of seeing themselves as adults and holding adult expectations of an employer. In return it asks that employers deal with individuals as adults.

☐ In making the deal that is right for you, there are four processes that need to be utilised by both parties. These are the gaining of information, the use of effective negotiation skills, the monitoring of change, and a willingness to renegotiate for change or exit with grace.

"Can't usually means won't."

part two
•••
making it work for you

" *Career management in the core no longer means waiting for someone to think on your behalf. It means using your reconnaissance to seize the initiative.* **"**

thriving in the core

> *'Most organisations have changed the employment contract with their employees, they just haven't told them so.'*
> Professor Ed Lawler III

Career management in the core no longer means waiting for someone to think on your behalf. It means using your reconnaissance to seize the initiative.

So you have decided that for the foreseeable future your place is in the core of the organisation. Before you read any further carry out this reality check on yourself:

● Is it because you cannot imagine it will be possible to find work elsewhere?

● Is it because you think your best chance of job security is by sticking with what you know?

● Is it because your career expectations can best be met by the opportunities emerging in your organisation (or another)?

If the first two explanations match your thoughts, then I've failed to convince you that the core is no longer a womb. In that case it's time to reread Chapter 3. If you accept the third explanation then read on.

A backlash is developing among knowledge workers about the demands of transactional contracting, and that backlash is now causing ripples among employers. When Roffey Park Management Institute questioned organisations about the impact of delayering on career management, they voiced considerable concerns:

● How do we retain good people when promotion prospects are reduced?

- How do we meet requirements for perceived progress and reward systems as a substitute for promotion increases?

- How do we demonstrate rewards are still there?

- How do we build credibility and morale?

- How do we convince staff that they have a career with the company?

You can sense disquiet and confusion in their comments. The organisations are struggling as much as individuals to find a way of making the idea of career meaningful in the future. They are edging towards the idea of new forms of contracting, but are unsure how to manage these new arrangements, which imply allowing for individual differences when organisational systems have been built on minimising differences and avoiding anomalies. Confusion is stopping them from signalling openly that the old deal is gone. It's important to recognise their anxiety, because it gives you an important piece of information – pure transacting doesn't work as a long-term tactic, because it doesn't deliver the goods for either side.

The psychological contract for those who remain in the core has to be based on interdependence and balance: interdependence as an acknowledgement that the goals of both are best served by working positively together; balance in the sense that the expectations of both parties receive acknowledgement and response.

● ● ● Your core career as a joint venture

A career in the core is a joint venture. Many joint ventures collapse because the needs of both parties are not sufficiently balanced to ensure an equality of investment and effort. Your core career will be a success if you give it the attention and investment of the best of joint ventures, and recognise when a particular venture is complete and it's time to renegotiate. If we examine the mutual interests in this joint venture, then we can focus on the balance you look to create:

"A career in the core is a joint venture."

Your interest is in remaining employable, whether within your present organisation, with another, or in the longer term as a peripheral worker.

Your interest is in knowing that your contribution is of value and that you are valued.

Your interest is in being involved in those activities which take the organisation forward, and not being involved in functions or assignments whose life cycle is coming to an end.

Your interest is in ensuring that you are constantly learning.

Their interest is in having employees who can and will contribute fully.

Their interest is in having employees who will flex and adapt to change, according to business need.

Their interest is in getting the best out of individuals.

Their interest is in having employees who demand to learn.

Their interest is in developing commitment, but without generating dependency.

Will loyalty matter any more?

In this joint venture, there is a potential balance of interests, but one phrase missing from both agendas is loyalty. Does it have a place in the future career contract? The death of loyalty has been a much commented on aspect of recent years, but what does loyalty mean? My dictionary defines it as personal devotion to a sovereign or would-be sovereign. Few of us would describe our relationship with our CEO in those terms. It implies a feudal exchange of submission for protection, or more positively an offering of affection and fidelity in return for meeting economic needs. It is at base an exchange of interests with recognised mutual responsibilities. From my childhood I remember Miss Smith, a housekeeper who looked after a father and son devotedly for thirty years. Her one night off was spent darning their socks and repairing shirt collars, because they were notoriously mean. When she retired in her 70s, to a home for single women, not once did they visit her. She offered unquestioning loyalty, but what did they offer in return, beyond pay?

The idea of loyalty to an organisation is difficult to understand. What is it that we are loyal to – corporate headquarters, the logo, the board? Loyalty is always to individuals, to our workmates, our boss, to doing the job as well as we can for our customers. It is based on valuing ongoing relationships. Why should this change with a new deal? Your new loyalty can be rooted in monitoring the give and take of key relationships rather than in abstract feudal terms. The Me Ltd school of thought would consider loyalty as misplaced in anyone but oneself. It's true that remaining true to oneself and one's values will be key to building a satisfying career in the future, but the idea of only showing loyalty to oneself rings warning bells of the amoral excesses of young financial dealers let loose in the City.

● ● ● Organisations still need loyalty

If loyalty still has a place in an individual psyche, then why not also in the organisation? Their actions over the last few years have branded them as disloyal. How could they get rid of that manager who has only ever given of his best, just because he's 50? How can they hand out 75 per cent pay rises at one end of the organisation and deny any pay rise at the other? How can they close down that operation, which is so central to the local economy? There's little point in offering loyalty if it isn't going to be matched with a suitable offering. Organisations are going to need to create a sense of loyalty if they are to attempt to achieve

"Organisations are going to need to create a sense of loyalty if they are to attempt to achieve more and more, with fewer and fewer."

more and more, with fewer and fewer. It's loyalty, at distribution company ADL that makes staff, regardless of role, work through the night in order to ensure that Sainsbury's get their goods on time at Christmas. It's loyalty that makes a chief executive accept a pay freeze along with his staff. For the future it's loyalty that should drive an organisation to ensure that for as long as a person is employed by them they will be developed and given challenges. Organisational loyalty could come to mean equipping you to be an independent and skilled individual who can leave the organisation confident of being able to be employed elsewhere. It's not loyalty in the sense of the nineteenth-century dynasties who built homes and art galleries for their employees, but it's a meaningful statement of commitment for the 1990s.

● ● ● Are you dejobbed?

Ironically, one of the casualties of being in the core will be your job. This may seem like nonsense. Your job has never been bigger, you have never given more time to it, and you've probably spent longer in it than any previous job. It seems as though you are welded to your job. You probably are, but you need to sever that connection if you are going to operate successfully. When Sundridge Park surveyed managers in 1993, they told us loudly that their job had more responsibility, more variety, sometimes more autonomy and certainly more challenge than when they first took it on. It was for those very reasons that they felt it was time for promotion. What we didn't recognise, as we empathised with their sense of grievance, was the truth that their job wasn't their job anymore. They were now operating in a world beyond their job description or, in the words of William Bridges they were 'dejobbed'. They were still looking at what they were doing against the job description to which they had been appointed and wanting recognition of those additions, instead of accepting that they now occupied a different job.

In my years in the public sector considerable time was spent in assessing whether what we were being asked to do was within our job description. If it wasn't it was grounds for complaint, 'that's not my job', or a speedy regrading application. The response was understandable under a rewards system which paid according to grade and length of time in post, rather than for performance or competences. Today the idea of the bounded job remains strong, even where performance related pay is the norm.

● ● ● Forget about the job and look at your jobs

Our response, argues Bridges, is based in the historical development of the job. In its origins it simply meant a task – moving a pile of hay, planting potatoes, moving goods from one place to another. A person's day would encompass a number of jobs, which would vary according to the season and weather. People did enough jobs in order to gain sufficient income to live, but they would not have described themselves as having a job. In a phrase which still survives, they would have talked about 'having a job on'. With industrialisation, that ease of choosing when to work and moving between jobs was reduced until in the twentieth century we translated job as a series of tasks, into job as an identity.

I never believe accounts of meetings with the rich and famous where the new romantic partner claims 'I never knew she/he was a world famous actor/singer/musician/politician, until long after we met.' The supposed subtext being, I was attracted by their own true worth, not their power, wealth and fame. In reality we know it is almost impossible to get through a casual social encounter, without at some point having our occupation unearthed. It places us in context, signals our income, our lifestyle, our social network, our values. No wonder losing one's job has such a powerful psychological impact, since it literally means taking away one's identity. Notice how guardedly professional people currently ask the 'what do you do?' question, because they fear exposing the loss of identity suggested by redundancy. If we haven't already literally lost our job, those in the core are going to have their job taken away from them. Instead core workers are going to be asked to:

● do anything necessary, in order to deliver the required results

● work to the core purpose of the job, i.e. why does this function exist rather than what does this function do

● deliver a skill set, which is linked to expected outcomes, and will change over time.

All of these uncertainties exist without there being any guarantee of promotion, although ability to deliver will attract financial recognition. Breaking the job/identity link will be a necessary condition for survival. It means a return to the origins of the idea of a job. We will have jobs to do, rather than having a job. We will do those jobs in order to remain in the arena which is the core, rather than doing them primarily in order to move upwards (although some still will). Our identity will come from the assignments we are involved with, the customers we work with, the skills we have acquired, and our perceived value to the organisation.

● ● ● Sustaining your value in a competitive market

One of the perks of working for a blue chip company was that they operated an internal labour market, which meant that from the earliest days of a career people knew who the competition was and how they stacked up against them. For the future there is no such thing as a purely internal labour market because the organisation has become 'boundaryless'. When a job has to be filled, a new function established, or a department restructured, the discussion will encompass not only whether we need 'outsiders' but do we want to commit to a permanent full-time employee.

Competition now comes from contractors, from those who will contract to deliver an outcome and then disappear when the job is over. As a core worker this means that you will constantly be in the marketplace, and will need to be utilising the skills you have used in selling yourself to a potential new employer to your present one. That is a considerable mind set shift. HR managers tell me that the weakest applications often come from internal candidates. On the assumption that since the employer knows them there is no point trying to sell themselves, or that since they know them allowance will be made, their applications are often so poorly presented that they would never attract interest elsewhere. They are seeing the organisation as family, and families accept each other's faults, don't they? Now we have established that the relational deal is over, core workers also have to market themselves. What's more they have to market themselves year on year, not just when applying for a new job. Since formal 'new jobs' will reduce in number, but work to be done will increase, it means constantly having to be aware of and developing your internal marketability.

"Now we have established that the relational deal is over, core workers also have to market themselves."

● ● ● Building marketability

Resistance to the idea of personal marketability is often strong. While it has appeal to those with a Get Ahead career driver, who spend time speaking up their achievements, and looking for networking opportunities with senior managers, it can seem pointless to those who believe that the organisation already knows them 'warts and all', or that self-marketing is unpalatable 'politicking'. In fact the organisation often doesn't know you well, just as you may know very little about it. It knows what you have been doing, but does it know what you have learnt? It knows what it has asked you to do since you joined, but does it know what skills you have used elsewhere? It knows what you can do, but does it know what you would value doing? Just as you may know what the organisation is involved in now, but what picture do you have of its medium-term future? You may know what is required in your function, but what do you know about what is happening in the same function in other business units, or even other functions in your business unit? Considering the investment in Management Information Systems, it is amazing how little information we have about each other. The first step towards increasing your marketability has to be based on **increasing your information base**.

YOU NEED TO KNOW ABOUT THE ORGANISATION		
Do you know?	*Yes*	*No*
What is the business strategy – often the hardest piece of information of all to acquire, though if it's not in the public domain how can you be expected to work to support it?	☐	☐
The key projects, on which future growth is being based?	☐	☐
What use of technology is making possible in terms of new products and services?	☐	☐
How planned new technologies will impact on resourcing?	☐	☐
What customer needs the organisation is most anxious to meet?	☐	☐
What abilities are being rewarded?	☐	☐

Do you know?	Yes	No
Where investment is being made?	☐	☐
What competitors are most admired/feared and what is it that they do that your organisation doesn't?	☐	☐
What customers they would most like to gain?	☐	☐
What legislation could impact/is impacting on business and how?	☐	☐
Where they are looking to create cost savings through re-engineering?	☐	☐
What is becoming less important to the organisation?	☐	☐
Where are jobs growing and shrinking?	☐	☐
The strength of the organisational skill base for dealing with new strategic areas?	☐	☐
How dependent the organisation is on outside contractors for delivering on key development projects?	☐	☐
Which functions and individuals seem to have most power in strategic decision making?	☐	☐
What are the priorities of key decision makers?	☐	☐
What is now expected of you?	☐	☐

If the answer to most of the questions is 'No', you are not alone. Professor Ed Lawler, of the University of Southern California regularly surveys the information provided by US Fortune 1000 companies. He reports that in 1993 only 24 per cent provided employees with information on competitors' performance and 31 per cent told employees about technologies that could affect their work. Just because the organisation isn't telling, doesn't mean you shouldn't be asking.

Not all of these questions will apply if you are working in the public or voluntary sectors, but there will be equivalent areas of enquiry which will help you identify the emerging organisational profile, and where you could fit into it. The underlying message of this line of enquiry is that marketability depends on keeping a close eye on the organisational agenda, and allying your career development to it. It also means recognising where there are skills gaps that no one is currently equipped to fill. No organisation can afford to be totally reliant on external contractors. It makes sense to be looking to transfer learning into the organisation, and growing the internal skill base. Don't reject possibilities because at the moment you do not have the particular skill. It will be an increasing feature of the future that no one will. It is through assignments that learning will grow.

THE ORGANISATION NEEDS TO KNOW ABOUT YOU

Do they know?

	Yes	No
Where you see your interests lying against the emerging future?	☐	☐
When you last had a discussion about how you see yourself contributing in the future, rather than whether you have met your objectives for the last year?	☐	☐
Where you want to develop your skills?	☐	☐
How you are prepared to develop? Do they know your preferences for course study, on the job learning, secondments, temporary assignments, distance learning?	☐	☐
How much of yourself you are willing to give to work?	☐	☐
Whether your marital status makes you more or less willing to relocate (or do they make assumptions on your behalf)?	☐	☐
Do they know what you have learnt in the past two years?	☐	☐
Do they know your career expectations?	☐	☐
Do they know what you have learnt from contacts with clients, customers and suppliers and how that might feed into new opportunities?	☐	☐
Do they know how flexible you are?	☐	☐

We assume our line manager knows our ambitions and desires, although when Peter Herriot and I questioned managers we discovered bosses were poor interpreters of their subordinates ambitions. Achieving a balance of interests and increasing our personal marketability relies on both being more curious than we have in the past about what's happening, but also telling others the answers to questions they might not have even thought to ask. If you wonder why you are seldom asked questions that could help your career, the answer is often because those who manage you fear they have nothing to offer, and so believe it is better not to open up the discussion. Career management in the core means no longer waiting for someone to think on your behalf. It means using your reconnaissance to seize the initiative. Rather than waiting for the market to come to you, you define your market.

● ● ● Jim Page: the reconnaissance agent

Jim Page has used his information gathering skills to open up a career area which he believes could sustain his career in the core for the next ten years. Starting life as a lecturer, he monitored changes in education policy and came to the conclusion that a career based on mere survival, teaching increasing student numbers with shrinking resources was not likely to sustain a sense of success. In his mid-thirties, he took the risk of giving up his job to return to college to complete an MSc conversion programme in computing. Given the skills shortages in IT this hardly seems a career risk, but to his colleagues the move seemed bizarre. 'Why give up a secure job to enter a completely new area where you will be competing against 21 year olds?' he was asked by well meaning friends. They were right in one sense, he was competing against 21 year olds, but he also had a belief that the interpersonal skills he had acquired would give him an edge in getting the job done, even if his technical skills didn't match with those of a computing sciences graduate.

This was the late 80s when house prices were dinner table talk, and credit was easy, so he deliberately targeted his job search at major credit card companies. He was fortunate that one offered him a job, and placed him on a graduate entry development programme alongside 22 year olds. Within a short time his personal skills began to win out against youth. He found himself working on international assignments where his ability to get along with people, and his earlier experiences as a psychologist helped him in achieving outcomes, and attracted speedy promotions. Within five years he was back on track against his peer group, but he was now operating in a very different business climate. Credit card companies had had their fingers burnt by the over extensions of the 80s, and the more sober 90s saw a reduction in consumer willingness to spend. At this point he assessed what he had learnt in the past years, and recognised that the cross-cultural projects he had been involved in gave him a firm background for working with a Europe-based company. A contact through a former colleague introduced him to a major European finance house, which offered him a job working with UK banks on IT projects.

This proved a steep learning curve as he found himself working with specialists with twenty years' banking experience, and commuting to Europe where his IT staff were based. After nearly two years, he felt on top of the job. He now knew he could manage complex assignments, with tight schedules and demanding clients. He knew he could learn quickly and get to grips with new areas of work in short periods of time. He knew he could prioritise and manage multiple demands without burning out in the process. He had learnt a lot about himself, and he had also learnt a lot about banking. It was becoming clear from observation and from reading the financial press that a new theme was emerging, the use of electronic purses as debit cards. The idea that, in order to minimise use of cash, customers will carry a 'smart card' which stores money downloaded on to a chip, to make small purchases. UK banks were testing the idea in pilot projects, but his own company was just starting out on the idea. The project was being worked on by external consultants and there seemed to be little expertise in-house. Rumour had it that staff would have to be headhunted from competitors who had a lead time advantage.

Rather than listen to the rumours, Jim decided to go and talk with the project head, to find out what was needed, and to let him know of his interest in being involved. He recognised he had little knowledge, but then it was clear that few others did. What he did have was a track record of achievement, of learning fast, of delivering, of managing multinational teams and of withstanding pressure. By the end of the discussion he knew that the project was vitally important to the organisation and that the current reliance on external contractors was not desirable. He also had copies of two job descriptions which had not been made public. By the next morning, based on his discussion, he was clear on what he could contribute, and also clear that neither job description accurately described what he felt needed to be done. By midday the Project Director had offered him a job and agreed that the job descriptions needed revision. They were now ready to start negotiating with each other on terms and conditions.

Is Jim exceptional in his abilities? He is certainly able, but no doubt there are others who could take on the role. What distinguishes him is his approach to career dealing, which constantly moves from the wider external framework – what is coming into view, to the micro environment, how can I find out what is available, and how can I sell myself in terms which meet their needs as well as my own? What Jim is doing, though he would never call himself a salesman is following a classic model of salesmanship. It's a model known as **CICPRODE**, which is frequently used in structuring the selling process. If we analyse Jim's process his use of **CICPRODE** is visible.

Curiosity	Jim was curious about what was happening in electronic transfer of funds, so he was a potential buyer of the idea of working in this new area.
	He was also a seller in that making the direct approach he was looking to raise the Project Director's curiosity in him.
Involvement	Having found out more about the project his desire to be involved grew.
	Having heard about his interest, the other party started to develop a sense of involvement with him, so that the idea of directly appointing rather than putting the vacancy out to a recruitment agency started to appeal.
Confidence	The speed with which the Project Director responded to his enquiry gave him confidence that he must have something to offer.
	Jim's encouragement of the Project Director to talk with those who have worked with him, and been responsible for him before taking any further steps, provided information which con-

firmed the confidence he had gained in the initial discussion.

Problems   Both openly addressed the problems which were likely to arise in an assignment of this type. The company has a lot riding on it, potentially a career could be made or broken by the outcome. They also both acknowledged the importance of getting the project moving quickly. There was no attempt by either side to minimise the problems which may be involved, including Jim's reluctance to relocate in the short term, because of his partner's career.

Resolution   The subsequent discussions have been ones of looking to create a deal which is workable from both perspectives. The mutuality of interest in making a workable solution has been transparent.

Objections   Those things which could stop a deal being made were aired. They included, from Jim's perspective, financial considerations and pressure to be based in Europe full time. From the organisation's it includes the time frame for starting. If Jim could not find a replacement for his present position swiftly, the immediate appeal of his CIC would begin to wane. It had earned him entry, but without the detail of the follow-up, it cannot ensure a satisfactory deal for both parties.

Decision   In this instance the decision almost preceded the resolution. The organisation showed its willingness early on to offer. In most deals the decision on both sides will only be made once the PRO has been dealt with.

Evaluation   In such a career deal there are two levels of evaluation. Does the contract meet both needs in the short term, but more importantly will the terms of the deal be met by both sides so that they would be willing to deal again? As I write, the second evaluation hasn't been made. It will only be possible once the project is completed. Then the organisation will know if it has gained the desired outcome. If it has then it will be willing to deal in the same way with Jim Page again. It will have monitored his performance, against the negotiated deal and decided if it was a fair one from their perspective. Did he deliver on time and on budget? Did he learn quickly enough to deal with the demands of the assignment? Did his demand that he was not immediately moved away from London cause problems for the project and his team members? Did he add value that couldn't have been gained from recruiting externally?

Jim too will have been monitoring the deal, and deciding whether to enter further negotiations. Did they give him enough resource that he was able to deliver on what was acknowledged as a demanding assignment? Did they give him sufficient support that he was stretched, but not overwhelmed? Did they accept that he wasn't always in corporate HQ, or did they drag him over from London for weeks on end? Did he acquire new skills that both retained his internal marketability and increased his external marketability? Was he given recognition for his contribution?

● ● ● How's your OTSW?

As a core employee you are also going to be in the process of selling yourself into new ideas, where your ability to manage the CICPRODE process will be an important part of your tool kit. The difference between the past and the future is that new jobs (as in pieces of work) are constantly going to become available, but the life expectancy of those jobs will often be short. One assessment is that already 65 per cent of jobs which now become available have never previously existed. These are jobs where there are no ideal candidates because no one skill set has been stamped on the post. They are open to being shaped around the skills and the developing skills of those people who are willing to CIC. As Patricia Ohlott and Marian Ruderman of the Center for Creative Leadership have shown, too often people assume that promotions come to those who fulfil the stated requirements of the next post, when in reality a candidate who can win the confidence of selectors will be allowed to shape the post around their own particular abilities. This will become increasingly so as job descriptions become obsolete.

Having information is key to managing, but there must be a balance of information about the organisation and yourself. There is no sales advantage if you understand where the organisation is going, but have little insight into yourself. In the next chapter we will be spending more time looking at your marketability, but for the moment there is one technique often used for looking at business opportunities which is equally appropriate for the career deal – SWOTing. The identification of strengths and weaknesses against current business opportunities, while simultaneously recognising those external threats which could prevent capitalising on opportunities, is a well established technique. However, marketing expert Gavin Barrett argues that a more useful, if less mnemonically attractive framework is OTSW. If we identify **future** opportunities and threats and then look at our own strengths and weaknesses against those futures, then we have a more useful instrument for self-evaluation than one which is solely based in the present. Applying the OTSW model to Jim Page, his profile could look like the one shown opposite.

Mapped out in this way the risk Jim Page's employers are taking is not as great as it first appears. There is clear potential gain in his involvement, and for an employee who places organisational membership and learning as high career expectations, the potential career pay-offs are self evident.

OPPORTUNITIES	THREATS
A new area of banking that is likely to be the single most significant change in personal finance this decade. Involvement in a new and complex area of IT. The chance to be in at the start of a major project, with no established experts within the company. A chance to make his reputation internally, through having a lead role in a pioneer project. A chance to increase his external marketability, since news of success will spread fast.	A high visibility assignment, whose failure could harm his career prospects inside and outside the company. Difficulty of managing expert consultants who will be more technically proficient. High pressure to deliver ahead of any competitor. The project may be so complex that it will not be realisable to deliver within the time frame set. A fact that will not be known until he has committed to involvement.

STRENGTHS	WEAKNESSES
A reputation for being able to project manage difficult assignments and demanding customers. The ability to motivate staff to deliver more than they think possible, and sometimes more than they should be asked to deliver. An ability to combine clear task focus and fine detail skills without losing sight of the people aspects of management. A track record in coming into new areas, often with little previous experience, and grasping the essentials quickly. An ability not to be phased out by lacking deep technological knowledge, while being able to manage those who have.	No previous experience of electronic banking. No previous experience of working on chip card technology

But what about you?

Having looked at the need to gather information on yourself and the organisation in order to build your marketability and start the CICPRODE process, it's time to develop your own OTSW. Fill in this page, or use an exercise book and answer these four questions:

What new opportunities are emerging in your organisation?	**What threats could either prevent your involvement or potentially harm your career?**
What skills do you have that build your case for involvement in those opportunities?	**What present weaknesses do you need to overcome in order to contribute fully?**

If you have problems in identifying your skills, then read Chapter 8 before completing the exercise. If you have problems in identifying your weaknesses I would be surprised, since experience tells me they roll off the pen with disturbing ease. If, however, you have difficulties in identifying opportunities or threats then you can go no further until you have spent time researching into what is happening in your organisation, your sector and your workplace. Without a strong information base it is impossible to create a new deal.

Remember

☐ Core workers can ensure a career deal that does not exploit them, provided that they view their career dealings as one of negotiation of mutual interdependence in which there is a balance of interest.

☐ Loyalty will still have a place in a core career but it will not be loyalty to an abstract concept of organisation. It will be loyalty towards doing a good job for your customers and loyalty to your team workers. If the conditions for doing a good job are removed, then loyalty will also die. For the organisation, loyalty should mean ensuring that time in the core does not make you organisationally dependent, and retains your external market value.

☐ Being in the core will mean being 'dejobbed'. You will need to replace the idea of job as your identity with the idea of work as a series of jobs that need to be done. Your identity will come from how well you achieve them, and how satisfying those assignments are.

☐ Marketability is going to come from increasing your knowledge of the organisation and increasing your knowledge of yourself.

☐ Using a sales model of CICPRODE can help you structure how you approach developing a new deal based on working with new opportunities and identifying problems which you may have recognised but others haven't.

☐ You don't need a SWOT, you need an OTSW. If you start from your current strengths and weaknesses, you are likely to look for opportunities which are already evident. If you start from new opportunities, you will find that strengths are transferable and weaknesses can be overcome.

"No one can guarantee that you will move up, it may not be possible to move across; but you have to be able to demonstrate to yourself and your employer, that you are moving forward.**"**

enhance the value of your core assets

'Your sense of job security lies in your employability.'
Apple Computer Company

How is your cv? Is it sitting in your pc ready to be updated when a headhunter calls, or that job advert you have been hoping for appears. When did you last update it? One, two, three years ago? Is it a lengthening list of dates and job titles or a professionally produced document of your achievements. Whatever it is, it's not the cv you now need. To carry on dealing in the core you need a new type of cv, one which builds daily, and which is focused not on getting you out, but on keeping you in, until you choose to get out.

● ● ● The core worker's cv

When I first started work, each week I would ask myself what have I done this week that I didn't do last week. The aim was to ensure that there was always a new experience to add to my repertoire. The achievements to external eyes would have been small – going to a meeting and speaking out, trying out something different with a client, initiating a conversation with someone I held in awe. I never mentioned this approach because I assumed everyone did the same. Over the years I have discovered that they do not, and that for some people the aim is to acquire the skills of the job as quickly as possible and to settle down to applying them without too much conscious thought (until they have to be repackaged and sold to the next employer). It's not that they are not learning, it's that they don't actively think about what they are learning. Do I need to say that this isn't enough? From now on your cv has to be living in the forefront of your mind every working day.

● ● ● Your asset-based cv

Think about the last year at work as if you were putting together a cv for a prospective employer. How would it read? My guess is that you would give an account of how you had spent your time. You would want to convince them that you had packed a lot into that year, so you would list the names of assignments you had been involved in, customers you have worked with, and responsibilities you have held. This records what you have been exposed to, and shows you have been diligent, but it doesn't tell:

● The measurable benefits of your involvement – are things being done more efficiently, is more work being sold, is there a better product or service?

● The qualitative benefits of your involvement – was the team able to function more effectively because of the role that you took in the project, are customers happier as a result of your contribution, were you able to bring in new ideas that would have been missing had you not been involved?

● What have you learnt during the past year? That will include knowledge, but more importantly the skills you have developed that can be transferred into other projects (projects which you might not even be aware of yet, and which may have a very different content than ones you have previously undertaken).

● Who have you worked with over the past year? If you haven't extended the range of people that you are in working contact with, both inside and outside the organisation, then your asset value will have started to decline.

● How is your department a better place as a result of your input over the last twelve months, and who would testify to it?

● If I asked to see your cv from two years previously, how different would it look from the one you have prepared for the last twelve months. If it bears strong similarities, then it's time to start disposing of some of your present assets, and to start acquiring some new ones.

Management guru Tom Peters, always a man to state his case strongly, argues that from now on we have to look at ourselves as capital assets. If an organisation writes off a piece of capital equipment over six years, then that is the likely life span of our capital assets to the organisation. We need to be aiming at development retooling every six years. If our piece of capital machinery is little different to what we offered six years ago, then we can expect to be vulnerable to disposal. Viewing yourself in this way gives a clear focus both for reviewing your experience and for setting your future development agenda. It means asking the sort of questions that Jim Page asked himself:

- What have I been doing, and achieving, and is it time I stopped doing it?

- What else is there that now needs to be done, and how am I equipped to do it?

- What evidence do I have that would convince someone that they should take a chance on me?

- What do I now need to learn in order that my assets increase, built on the foundations of what I have achieved to date?

- What is the relative value of the assets in my portfolio. Are some in decline, because the demand for them is reducing, but are there others that should now be placed at the front of the portfolio, though previously they attracted little interest?

The aim is to separate you from what you are doing, in order to focus on what you are acquiring. Build your own cv for the past year by following this process:

List the projects/jobs you have been involved with over the past year.
-
-
-
-

For each of them identify the skills which you used in contributing to those pieces of work.
-
-
-
-

Don't be restrained by the amount of space given on the page, use more paper to fully to explore your skills. As you identify them don't just focus on the hard quantifiable ones, consider the qualitative ones, the lubricant skills that helped get a job done. The fact that you can work with difficult people, know how to get things done the 'unofficial way', can read the pulse of the organisation's priorities, can get a team of people to pull together, or can resolve conflicts. If you find identifying skills difficult (and many do) then keep asking yourself, 'In order to do that job, what did I have to do?' Simply list the actions you had to take, in as much detail as you can remember. Then look at the list as a dispassionate outsider and ask what sort of abilities would someone need in order to be able to do those things? It's likely that a large number of those abilities relate to your personal skills, as much as any specific job knowledge.

> **"Reviewing your asset-based cv should be a quarterly event."**

● ● ● Review your skills

Armed with your list, you are then in a position to review:

- ● Is your list one which indicates skills which are so specific to your organisation, that they would have limited value elsewhere? **Is this a danger sign?**

- ● Is your list one which highlights that technical knowledge is a reducing part of your portfolio? **Is this a danger sign?**

- ● Is your list high on technical skills but low on lubricant skills? **This is a danger sign.**

- ● Does your list highlight that you have been developing in ways which balance and build your portfolio? **This should be your aim.**

- ● Does your list highlight that your skills are transferable outside of your organisation, and even your sector? **This should boost your confidence.**

Reviewing your asset-based cv should be a quarterly event. As business moves faster and faster, a year is too long without active reflection. Your cv is no longer a monument to what has passed, it is a catalyst for identifying what needs to be done. The public cv you present to a prospective employer is your marketing document, it is there to attract their curiosity, involvement and confidence. The assets

> **Your cv is no longer a monument to what has passed, it is a catalyst for identifying what needs to be done.**

cv which you prepare quarterly for yourself, has a different purpose. It is to keep you on track so that you have a sustainable position in the core. It is for review, in order that you can plan the next quarter proactively. It is not for public disclosure because it is where you ask the difficult questions of yourself:

● Not what did I do, but what would have helped me do it better?

● Not how do I explain that away, but how can I prevent it happening again?

● Not this is what I did, but would I want to do that again – would I learn anything from carrying out a similar assignment, or is it important not to?

● What isn't in my quarterly report that should be if I am going to be on track against what is going on around me?

It's development time

Your asset-based cv is going to be the basis of your development plan, another key element in retaining your position in the core. From now on, simply reviewing what you have learnt will not be enough, you will need to be defining what you have to learn. Your decisions on which jobs to become involved in should be based on proactively identifying

> **Development is too often serendipity when it should be proactivity.**

what would be learnt from doing that job, and monitoring whether you are acquiring that learning. Think of the jobs you are presently doing, what things could you be learning that so far you have given insufficient attention to? Development is too often serendipity when it should be proactivity. Development

Consultants Bryan Smith and Grahame Morphey have collected data from hundreds of managers by asking them about how they learnt from challenges. In almost all cases, individuals report that their learning came through post-hoc reflection. In very few cases did individuals prepare themselves for the next challenge by consciously looking to apply what they had learnt in the past, and in even fewer did they identify what they could learn from working through the difficulty. This held true whether it was working with a notoriously difficult boss, moving into a new job, or taking on a new assignment.

● ● ● How do you need to develop?

There's no blueprint for how core workers are going to need to develop. Each one of us has an individual skills profile, but developing your individual plan will require a combination of approaches:

● You need to hold on to your sense of what are your career expectations – they will give you a compass direction on where you should be looking for your development cues.

● You need to be reading market trends – what types of skill are gaining in value to your organisation, and your sector.

● You need to be acquiring skills in selling ideas. When training departments are being disbanded and the new mantra is self-development, it demands that you are proactive in identifying your development needs, and then selling the case.

● You need to be identifying the person/people who are gatekeepers to your acquiring the appropriate development. This may no longer be Personnel, it may no longer be your line manager. Who has the power to be sold your ideas and to give you what you need in return?

The climate is right for a more differentiated approach to development. Companies are abandoning a sheep dip approach where everyone at that level attends set courses with little assessment of their appro-priateness, or the learning outcomes. If you are lucky you may have a personal development plan set for you each year. If you are even luckier it is delivered. The difference between any company development plan and your own is that the former is largely set in the present of what needs

to be done, while your development plan needs to be equally
focused on the future. What do I
need to be able to do in order to
achieve the career rewards which

"Companies are abandoning a sheep dip approach."

I seek? Approaching development in this way creates a mind
shift. Lateral job moves become means of acquiring skills that
could open up new possibilities, rather than public signals of
plateauing. Paul Davies, HR Development Manager for 3M
(Europe), believes, 'It's a very rare person who makes two or
three lateral moves and makes no career progression as a result'
– provided that those moves are planned from a learning
perspective. If we look at two groups who want to stay in the
core, two very different approaches to development emerge.

● ● ● So you still want to be a senior manager?

Regardless of how flat the structure may seem, unless you are
working in a co-operative, there will still be some form of
hierarchy and someone will end up at the top of it. For someone
who still wants to be in the race, has career expectations high on
organisational membership, competition and management, how
are they going to need to develop? We'll assume that they know
all the traditional organisational careerist management
techniques. They have been on visible assignments, acquired a
mentor, and have changed organisation and function frequently.
They have ensured that they have been on the development
programmes associated with high flyers. They have given a high
time commitment, often to the detriment of their personal lives.
They have done the 'right things', but will it make it come right
for them? Are they developed for the conditions of the 1980s or
the twenty-first century. Through surveying nearly 300 Chief
Executives in 1993, I discovered what they thought their
successors would need in order to work with the business
conditions of the future. Their list may surprise you. They saw
senior managers as fulfilling roles of:

● Helper
● Ally
● Truster

- Citizen
- Networker
- Changer

Those who are setting the future strategic direction of their companies were acknowledging that doing business in the next decade is going to be fundamentally different. Organisations are unlikely to be able to succeed without working with competitors, suppliers and customers as allies. They are going to have to help individuals to achieve goals without being able to control what they do directly. They are going to have to answer to customers who are challenging on ethical issues as to how business is managed. They are going to have to guide their organisations through constant change by offering clear leadership and communicating with and listening to staff, rather than issuing instructions and vision statements.

When these findings were first shared with middle managers they were dismissive of this 'soft' stuff. They missed the point. This isn't a substitute for the company 'hardball' (it will be assumed that those skills are in place) or PR gloss, it's an admission that learning how to handle the less quantifiable is key to delivering on the quantifiable. Career Management Consultants GHN have also surveyed future top managers. They add intelligence, entrepreneurship and presentation skills to the list, and reported that senior managers are still unwilling to recognise that they need help in managing teams, interpersonal relationships, communication and responding more flexibly. Since you have development time ahead, if you want to be near the top, identify where your development needs are against this future scenario. Have you spent so much time delivering on results that you have given insufficient time to developing your people management skills? Have you succeeded as a solo operator and ignored your need to work within teams? Or have you spent your time doing a good job, but failed to acquire the skills in presenting a good job well? If you are wanting a long-term organisational career, then your development has both to equip you for delivering on the present, while keeping a development eye on the future. Is your need to start thinking 'soft?'

●●● What if you just want to retain your place in the core?

What about the rest who don't aspire to be Chief Executive, but like being part of an organisation and believe it offers the best arena for their skills. They like being a manager, or have a professional identity which they want to retain? Is there still a place for the company worker? The answer is yes, provided that development is in line with organisational values. It may result in the skills of the two once distinct groups crossing over. As more and more work is done by better educated and trained staff, who do not expect to be managed, in the sense of ensuring that they do their work, many middle managers will find that their best security comes from returning to use the functional skills which first brought them to attention. For them, development could mean 'returning to school' to discover what's changed since last time they worked as a specialist on a problem – letting go, through encouraging another team member to manage the project while they focus on their technical input. For other managers, their role is in transition, as their most highly valued skills become coaching younger colleagues or managing the commitment and performance of contractors, teleworkers and temporary hires. For them, development could mean 360 degree feedback on their interpersonal skills and paying greater attention to their role of leader and less to that of manager.

●●● The professionals

For professionals, development can mean a complete re-engineering of their mind set. They have seen enough specialist functions outsourced to know that they have to earn their place in the core by daily demonstrating their understanding of the competitive realities of the marketplace and their acceptance of business priorities. Identifying development needs for an engineer, accountant or HR specialist means asking some tough questions:

● How well do I compare with external specialists that I encounter? What skills do they offer that I don't have?

● How up to date am I are on best practice in my profession and on its application in other organisations?

135

- If I was made redundant and had to sell myself back to the organisation as a self-employed contractor, what skills would I be selling them, and would they be ones which are relevant to the business? How confident am I that they would buy me?

- What distinct contribution do I make to the competitive position of my organisation?

- Do I understand how this business operates?

- Do I regularly work with a range of other functions outside of my specialism, or do I operate within a peripheral ghetto?

- Do I find value and learning in the perspectives of colleagues who come from other disciplines?

For professionals development means broadening out, letting go of the protective armour of a professional identity as a separation between themselves and business functions, while continuously enhancing their professional skills. It could mean asking for a secondment into a business area, being physically moved out into the business area that they support, spending more time talking with colleagues with whom they do not share a professional identity, going out with sales staff to meet customers, or attending a financial management programme.

Whether looking to move up or to stay in the middle, you need to be addressing your development needs, not from the position of what would I like to learn, but from a position of what do I have to acquire in order to earn my right to be where I am, and where the organisation is going?

It doesn't have to cost

If your response to this is but there isn't a training budget, then the truth is that for most people there doesn't need to be. When I asked 200 managers in an international food and drinks company about their most important development activity, only a handful mentioned a course. Most talked about challenges that they had been involved with: being sent overseas to work within a very different culture; being thrown in at the deep end in a new job; working with more senior colleagues on an

"To develop means to bring out what is latent or potential."

acquisition; or starting up a new business area that they saw as key learning experiences. To develop means to bring out what is latent or potential – no one ever said that this only happened in a classroom, which doesn't mean you won't benefit from courses. They have a place in a planned development portfolio, but they are only one way of learning.

One certainty is that your core value is based on your continuous development, so now is the time to identify:

● What are your motives for being in the core, and what does this imply for how you need to develop?

● Should you be looking to move around rather than only focusing on moving up?

● How do you develop best? Do you like being thrown in at the deep end, and learning from action, or do you feel more comfortable with a learning input prior to testing it out in action? Do you like learning by yourself, or do you learn best when you are with others working through a task?

● What opportunities are there for developing in the ways you believe you need to? If those opportunities are not visibly on offer, who would you need to persuade to give you that opportunity?

● What two development actions would best support your continued place in the core?

●●● The organisation's part in developing your core value?

I've put so much emphasis on your role in retaining your place in the core that there's a danger we'll lose sight of the fact that the organisation has to ensure you can operate effectively. The offerings which you are making are continuously to increase the value of your investment, to develop in line with organisational need, to be responsive to changes in priority, and consciously and proactively to learn. Do all this and they are getting a good return on their investment in you, but what do they need to offer you in return?

TEN OFFERINGS THAT YOU SHOULD EXPECT FROM AN ORGANISATION?

1 To be clear on the organisation's purposes and on where your input fits into those purposes? If it doesn't then you need to renegotiate your role.

2 To be clear on what is expected of you and how your performance will be judged? If you are not given a perform-ance framework, then you'll create your own according to your own personal agenda, not theirs.

3 To be given the resources necessary to carry out your jobs? Of course there will never be enough people or money, but that shouldn't stop you asking for or expecting resources of information, authority, support and time.

4 To be given adequate rewards that recognise your skills, learning performance and commitment. These rewards should be ones that you value – which may be different from the rewards which others value.

5 To be told when you are doing a good job, and when you are not.

6 That your development will be taken seriously as a business performance issue, and that a range of development options will be available.

7 To be shown that you do matter, that you are not merely a capital asset, but a human one as well. This does not mean a return to paternalism, it's sound business etiquette.

8 To be given the responsibilities of being in the core and freedom in how you achieve your objectives.

9 That the organisation will not consciously inflict stress through denying you a sense of control over your work; failing to provide support and overwhelming you with demands. The law has now established that employers have a duty of care for employees. Making employees ill through the demands placed on them is not legally acceptable.

10 A sense of security, contingent on your delivering your part of the deal. If your employer can make no long-term promises on job security, you should expect that they are tending your security in the wider job market.

You may disagree with this list, it may seem idealistic, fail to capture what you are seeking, or to reflect the state of play in your organisation. **You** are the architect of your career deal. Now you know what is going to be expected of you, recognise for yourself the deal you should be seeking.

TO OPERATE AS THE CORE WORKER I WANT TO BE:	
I need to be able to offer ...	**From my organisation I will expect ...**
●	●
●	●
●	●
●	●
●	●
The organisation will expect of me ...	**The organisation will need to offer me ...**
●	●
●	●
●	●
●	●
●	●

Looked at in this way, are you offering enough to sustain your place in the core? If you are not then it's time to do some work on your asset value. If the organisation is not offering enough to compensate for your input, then it's time to start to renegotiate the deal (see Chapter 13) or to look for another employer.

Remember

☐ Maintaining your position in the core means continuously updating your asset-based cv, both as part of your record of achievement, and as a diagnostic tool for where you should be building your skills.

☐ Maintaining the value of your portfolio is going to be based on continuously learning and recognising when it's time to retool.

☐ You are going to need to define your individual development agenda based on where and how you see yourself operating in the core, and the organisation's business agenda.

☐ Giving all this attention to increasing the value of your offerings means that you should also be defining the offerings you need from the organisation.

☐ No one can guarantee that you will move up, it may not be possible to move across, but you have to be able to demonstrate to yourself and your employer that you are moving forward.

" The mark of a peripheral worker is that they operate as a verb rather than a noun. Peripheral working is about doing. "

living on the edge

'*By 2001 self-employment will represent over 13 per cent of all employment.*'
Labour Market Trends 1995-6

The changing deal within the core is being driven by the need to give organisations the functional flexibility they need to meet changing competitive conditions. The growth of the periphery is being driven by a desire for numerical flexibility and cost control on head count. There is nothing new in this. What's new is that it is now impacting on professional employees. We have long been used to the temporary secretary, the agency cleaner and the outside security firm, but the shift of peripheral working up the organisational structure is a phenomenon of the 1990s. The key for career dealers looking towards the periphery is to find those areas where the organisation focus is on acquiring high added value and away from those areas where the organisation is primarily using 'just-in-time' as a technique to cost control staff resourcing.

International management consultancy PA sees the peripheral market as being as stratified as an organisational pyramid. The nearer the top an individual's input influences, the stronger is the individual's negotiating hand. The closer to the bottom, the more open the individual is to exploitation as the price of gaining a measure of continuity.

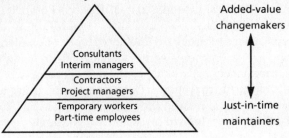

If contingent working is to offer satisfaction rather than exploit-ation, then those who choose or are forced to operate at the periphery have to work on gaining the best deal they can.

● ● ● What makes for success at the periphery?

In the 1980s, career management consultancy Drake Beam Morin established through workshops with entrepreneurs consistent themes in their success:

- A willingness to **accept responsibility and accountability** because they believed that given freedom, they could do the job better than others.

- A level of **self-confidence** which enabled them to be dogged in pursuit of objectives.

- A constant sense of urgency and an enjoyment of **thriving on activity**.

- A strong sense of **realism** which enabled them to deal with situations as they were, rather than working with ideals. They were able to **flex** in response to need.

- An **ability to work in ambiguous situations** and to find patterns and links which enabled them to find a way through.

- **A low need for symbols of status**, because their own business performance was their most valued status symbol.

- An **objective view of relationships**, which focused on what people could accomplish.

- The **emotional stability** to handle pressures and to control emotions, so that they did not interfere with business progress.

- Attraction to **challenge**, rather than seeing it as high risk.

Looked at from the 1990s there is little here that would not appear on an organisational list of desired competences. The language of flexibility, responsibility, accountability and auto-nomy, resistance to pressure and acceptance of challenge is now common in assessment centres designed to identify high-potential managers. The skills of the entrepreneur have become the skills of the 'intrapreneur'. Does that mean we are all equally capable of living a career on the organisational edge? The answer has to be 'No'. An individual who may willingly accept these

demands as part of the exchange in a corporate career may feel
ill equipped to apply them externally. The issue is not one of
competence, it's about fit with the tacit demands of living as an
autonomous worker, dimensions which are often not visible until
the life is led.

● ● ● The autonomy audit

Start to make your own assessment of your present level of
comfort with the demands of living on the edge, through
completing the autonomy audit. For the moment ignore the last
column, and decide the level of importance which you attach to
each of the following statements.

THE AUTONOMY AUDIT

Section 1 *How important as an* **encourager** *towards becoming self-employed are the following?*	Very important 3	Some importance 2	No importance 1	Extra weightings
1 Stepping outside the working norms of an organisation				
2 Knowing you would have full accountability for the results of your work				
3 Believing that you could earn more than as an employee				
4 The opportunity to build a wider reputation for your skills				
5 Having job security/insecurity in your own hands				

	Very important 3	Some importance 2	No importance 1	Extra weightings
6 Believing that you are the best assessor of how well or badly you perform a job				
7 Believing that you have abilities which are not being fully utilised				
8 Being able to work alone				
9 Having a network of friends and former colleagues who are now self-employed				
10 The prospect of being your own organisation, in total control of quality in every aspect of the business				
11 Being able to give 110% to your own work				
12 The contrast between intense working time, and time without work for following other interests				
13 The opportunity to take a risk with your life				
14 The possibility of creating your own organisation where you could manage others according to your own principles				
15 Seeing a direct relationship between your ability to sell your skills and your income				

	Very important 3	Some importance 2	No importance 1	Extra weightings
16 Believing you could market yourself				
17 The opportunity of working with a number of organisations rather than being tied to one				
18 Letting go of an organisational career				
Total				

Section 2 *How important as a* **dissuader** *from becoming self-employed are the following?*	Very important 3	Some importance 2	No importance 1	Extra weightings
19 A lack of an imposed structure to the working day				
20 Knowing that you would carry the total blame for mistakes				
21 Fear that your financial security will be at risk				
22 Fear that your personal reputation will be at risk				
23 The high price you put on security within the rewards package you seek				
24 The lack of feedback mechanisms (except financial) on how well you are doing				

	Very important 3	Some importance 2	No importance 1	Extra weightings
25 Having to be your own encourager and performance coach				
26 Fear that working from home will be lonely				
27 Concern about being able to build a social element into working life, when no longer attached to an organisation				
28 The thought of having to be everything from MD to cleaner, purchasing manager to machine fixer				
29 Knowing that keeping work and life demands in balance will be impossible at times				
30 Lack of control over the flow of work				
31 Having to constantly build new relationships with clients				
32 Being financially responsible for employees				
33 Having your income depend on your ability to sell yourself				
34 Having to give at least 25% of your time to marketing rather than delivering				

	Very important 3	Some importance 2	No importance 1	Extra weightings
35 Knowing there are areas of running a business in which you have little knowledge or confidence				
36 The lack of a clear career future				
Total				

● ● ● Revisit the audit

Having totalled Sections 1 and 2 separately, you now have the opportunity to give weightings to those items which are of most importance to you. You have an **additional 20 points** to divide between the **very important** items in **both** parts of the audit.

For example: While you may have identified a number of encouragers, they may be outweighed by the single fear of exposing yourself to financial risk. In this case you would allocate all 20 points to question 21.

Or: here may be 2 or 3 encouragers that would drive you through against an even longer list of discouragers. Allocate your points between those encouragers.

> You now have your **Autonomy Balance Sheet**
>
> (Total questions 1–18 + weightings) –
> (Total questions 19–36 + weightings)
> Balance: +
>   –

The balance of your motivators over your dissuaders gives you a first indication of how prepared you are to move to the edge. The higher the positive score, the more you recognise inherent satisfactions in the possibility of autonomy, which outweigh the uncertainties which every self-employed person has to live with. The higher the negative score, the more the offerings that come with organisation-based work carry importance in your personal contract. If your score is evenly balanced, then like most people currently entering self-employment, there is a wavering pull and push between the impulse for security and the impulse for self-direction. Natural entrepreneurs won't need the autonomy audit, the strength of their self-belief that they have something to offer will override any negative thoughts. Many of those now finding themselves living at the edge would not previously have seen themselves as entrepreneurs. It has been forced on them, or they have come to it as a better option than a continued organisational life. They come with reservations and self-doubt. Those who make a success of the shift are those who work on reducing the restrainers.

● ● ● Weaken your restrainers

In completing the questionnaire you have recognised that there is a force field operating around you:

● The encouragers which are driving you towards change.
● The dissuaders which are pushing you back.
● Particular encouragers which could have sufficient strength to help you overcome obstacles.
● Particular restrainers which could repel any driving force.

In looking again at your list of discouragers are there any which with some thought could become a positive force? For example:

Discouragers	Levers for reducing discouragement
● Lack all the areas of expertise needed to run your own business. ● Fear loneliness of working alone.	● Work in partnership with others. ● Establish associate links with other freelancers, not only to share work, but also to offer support and advice.
● Lack of support and feedback. ● Dislike of self-marketing and the time it takes.	● Subcontract your time to an established contractor. ● Link up with a recruitment consultancy for interim management assignments.

Discouragers	Levers for Reducing Discouragement
● Fear of unpredictable fluctuations in demand for your work.	● Find at least one client where you will accept a lower pay rate in exchange for a commitment to ongoing work.
● Dislike of continuously having to build new relationships with clients.	● Opt for working as a contractor on long-term assignments.

With thought, those things which look the biggest barriers can become levers in a successful move towards the edge. Look back over your audit and reassess your force field:

● What could you do that would maximise your encouragers?

● What could you do to turn your restrainers into drivers?

● Do you now feel more comfortable about the possibilities of life on the periphery? If the answer is 'No', then turn to Chapters 7 and 8, to assess yourself against what organisational membership will require of you. If the answer is 'Yes', then carry on reading.

●●● Reading the barometer

Underpinning the audit are important barometric readings on your ability to live the life of an autonomous worker:

● Willingness to accept a life which will at times involve longer working hours than were ever experienced in an organisation. Those who leave an organisation with a personal agenda of gaining life balance through self-employment are often disappointed. More realistic for knowledge workers is an acceptance of a continuous trade off between income gained and time gained. The key to balance is judging when a client meeting wins out over attending a child's school event, or the need for a holiday wins out over accepting another piece of work.

● Acceptance of the responsibilities that accompany autonomy.

Responsibility not just for income, but for the quality of the work produced, mistakes made and for acting as one's own coach and encourager.

- Acceptance of risk, because of a belief that one's abilities reduce the odds of failure.

- Ability to self-critique positively as a means of improving delivery not destroying confidence.

- The emotional resourcefulness to flex with the pressures of overdemand and the potential stress of underdemand.

- A conscious attention to providing those social and emotional aspects of working life which do not come as part of the self-employed package. It is no accident that good health is a known marker of successful entrepreneurs. They often give considerable attention to ensuring they remain healthy through looking after their physical, emotional and social health.

- A willingness to do whatever is necessary, without casting an eye backwards to the days when support functions freed you to address the core of your function. As a self-employed person every aspect of what you do is core.

- Comfort with projecting your own sense of identity as your marketing tool, rather than marketing yourself via a company name.

● ● ● Choices at the periphery

If the audit has convinced you that there is a comfortable place for you outside the organisation, then there is still a need to identify where you wish to locate yourself. This choice will be led by the skills which you bring and the expectations which you hold.

Expectation	Opportunities	Risks
Life-style balance	Just-in-time jobs	No training. Pay can be exploitative. Little skills development.
Expertise	Contracting	Repetitive assignments. Lack of training.

Expectation	Opportunities	Risks
		Value of specialist skills may decline over time.
Expertise Continuity	Consultancy	Organisations may want skills but restrict their application because of cultural factors or internal politics.
Expertise Challenge Management Freedom	Interim Management	Input may be undermined by the threat posed to existing managers.

Each of the deals brings with it potential risks which can undermine its attractions. There is evidence from the USA that the productivity gains which organisations believed they would gain from motivated self-employed 'temps' are not being found, because failure to provide training and support is undermining performance. Asking for training in order to help the organisation sustain quality and productivity could be part of a life-balancer's deal. Similarly Jone Pearce looking at contract workers in the USA has found they can become organisational 'Luddites', delivering skills which are increasingly outdated, because they have not invested in their own development. Seeing yourself as a capital investment that has to be continuously upgraded is central to delivering on the contractor deal. For those operating at the top of organisations the risks are often cultural and interpersonal. Skill in agreeing the terms of operation and establishing internal support systems are key to making these deals operable.

There is a further distinction between the matches, in that the more complex the expectations the more intrinsic are the satisfactions that are being sought. Where a life-balance employee may see work as a means of supporting the rest of their life, and the contractor may see high earnings as compensation for a marginalised role, those who choose consultancy and interim management are looking for opportunities to influence change (and earnings that reflect their ability to do so).

● ● ● The consultancy deal

William Morin and James Cabrera define a consultant as 'an expert adviser brought in from outside an organisation, to help solve problems in exchange for a fee'. A consultant is expected to offer:

● **Expertise** To have area(s) of technical expertise that are better developed than in those working within the organisation.

● **Advice** To be able to analyse situations and offer solutions; gaining acceptance through influence not authority.

● **An external world** To have a broader view that can be brought to bear on the client organisation.

The consultant is expected to offer both strong technical and interpersonal skills. They not only have to be credible in having a level of expertise that justifies their fee, they also have to be able to make everyone they deal with feel confidence and comfort in working with them. They have to be able to gain the trust of those who will help them understand the real nature of the problem they have been set, while also building good relationships with those senior managers who have to buy into and implement any recommendation they make. Implicit to these offers are:

● Professionalism in every aspect of their dealings with the client, from appearance to punctuality, speed of response to enthusiasm for the task.

● Strong communication skills, which enable their ideas to be understood by non-experts.

● Organisational sensitivity in how they operate and present their ideas.

● Trustworthiness, so that the client can have confidence that information will not be revealed to outsiders.

● An ability to offer realistic solutions, which will make a demonstrable difference and make their fees justifiable.

● A quality of output that gives confidence in building an ongoing relationship.

Clients are demanding in their expectations, but what about the deal from the consultant's perspective? A benefit of the consultant's life is that different deals can be sought from different clients. The same individual may seek an identification of values with one client, while another offers exciting assign-ments and a third offers the prestige of a well-known name that can be used for promotional purposes. There are, however, some offerings which most consultants will seek. The ability of a consultant to attract high rates is directly related to the speed at which they learn ahead of their clients. Assignments which provide stretch will be taken with enthusiasm, but the ability to maximise that learning will depend on the willingness of the organisation to allow challenge. The organisation that invites in a consultant, only to constrain them at every turn, resisting any challenge to existing thinking, not only wastes money but limits the contribution which could be made. Similarly the consultant who is denied information, denied access and denied acceptance will be unable to apply their expertise. A balanced deal that meets the need of both parties could look something like this:

Organisation expects ...	Consultant expects ...
High technical expertise that cannot be found within the organisation.	To be given freedom in how they work.
Strong interpersonal skills.	To be trusted by the client.
A sense of confidence in the ability and commitment of the consultant.	To be constantly learning from assignments.
Visible added value.	To add to the value of their portfolio of experience.
Confidentiality.	To be remunerated commensurate with their skills.
To feel comfortable with the fees paid, because of the quality of the input and output given by the consultant.	To build good client relationships that will lead to further work.

Organisation offers ...	Consultant offers ...
To let the consultant operate in ways that enable them to be effective, and which may be outside the organisational norms.	To work whatever hours are necessary in order to do the job as well as they can.
To include the consultant in organisational events, so that their knowledge of the organisation is cultural as well as technical.	To act in ways which are sensitive to the culture of the organisation.
	To be completely professional in their dealings with the client.
To give access to relevant information and individuals.	To give regular attention to their own development, both technically and personally.
To be challenged in their thinking.	To justify the fees charged.
To give feedback.	To see an assignment as the start of a relationship, not a 'cut and run' fix.

If you are considering working in a consultancy role, then you need to start identifying what is the deal you are seeking. What are you willing to offer, and what are you wanting in return? What are the risks you face, and how will you overcome them? It doesn't have to look like this deal, but it does need to be based around those things which you seek in order to operate as your best self. Recognising what you are offering and wanting will also lead you to consider the type of organisations you would want to deal with. It may even lead you, like Phil Bunnell, to build different deals with different clients.

● ● ● Phil Bunnell: a multiple dealer

Phil Bunnell stepped out of the security of working with a major building society in the early 80s and he's been living a peripheral life ever since. At the time leaving the most secure of employment areas for the relative insecurity of self-employment would have marked him out from his managerial colleagues, but it's a decision he has never regretted. Accepting redundancy instead of relocation, gave him the opportunity, but the process began during the previous two years when his view of the possibilities of work was influenced by two events. Appointed to head up the society's external projects, he had become involved in offering his organisation's expertise to projects concerned with unemployment and community regeneration. He was working outside the organisation, meeting people he had never encountered before and being stimulated by what he found. At the same time he was completing a Master's degree, and with two fellow students had set up a consultancy, to which he contributed in his spare time.

When he left employment he assumed this was the end of his involvement with 'business in the community', but instead two charities where he had been acting as a board member asked him to stay on. He has worked with them ever since. Both are companies with charitable status. One is concerned with environmental improvement in the north and midlands, the other with unemployment on the Wirral. Both have offered Phil considerable development. He has learnt to work with people from very different backgrounds to his own. He has been exposed to a full range of business issues, ranging from the strategic to the specific. In the process he has seen his confidence and vision grow. The experience he has gained has more than paid back the two or three days of unpaid time he gives each month.

Consultancy work has been the central core of his activity in the last thirteen years. Specialising in advising organisations on how to reduce the risks of mistakes and errors through focusing on human factors, the HEB Partnership has found a niche area where there are few competitors. Assignments can involve systematic investigations into why an assembly process is failing, why a design specification is inadequate or why errors of judgement are occurring. In the last two years a third theme has been added to his working life. He now works two or three days a month within the Management School of Thames Valley University, as well as acting as a tutor for the Open University.

Ask Phil what he gets from each of these different themes in his life and there are clear differentiations. Board membership gives him a global perspective on business issues. Consultancy offers the intellectual challenge of understanding a situation, presenting options and following their implementation. While in his teaching he enjoys the regular working contact with students, and the opportunity of offering and receiving new perspectives.

companies with charitable status, chief executives get an external sounding board, and someone who has a rich range of experiences which he can bring to debate. In his consultancy work clients receive plausible analysis, realistic recommendations and deliverable solutions. In his academic role, he is expected to bring his knowledge of organisational life, and an ability to establish credibility and good relationships with individuals and groups. If the three discrete lives sometimes cause problems of time management, conceptually he finds they reinforce each other, with crossover benefits between all three.

Phil did not set out with an aim of a tripartite life, neither did he leave employment with a firm conviction that he would never work as a permanent employee again. While in retrospect it is easy to talk in terms of seeking freedom or challenge, at the time he was simply excited at the immediate prospect of being his own boss. He was not seeking life balance, nor was money a prime motive. The last thirteen years have had their financial ups and downs, but he finds it difficult to imagine going back into an organisational career, unless he could be offered the variety and autonomy he has now come to expect. A decade on, the secure world he was once part of is no longer so secure. Where former colleagues are now feeling a loss of career control, his ability to pick up the phone to seek work gives him a firmer sense of control over his future.

●●● The interim deal – what is it?

Interim management would not have existed as a peripheral option within the UK ten years ago. Now it is a business with a 40 per cent annual growth rate. Where the talk was once of headhunting, now recruitment consultancies talk of 'head renting' – acting as agents for experienced managers who want to sell their managerial skills to a client on a short-term basis. If consultants are excited by new problems to which they can bring analytic skills, interim managers want to take it a step further by living with the organisation through the change process. The key difference, according to Julie Candlish, Principal Consultant of Interim Management at PA, is that they are 'temps' who are there to ensure change. Typical assignments could include turning a company around in preparation for its sale, merging two departments after an acquisition, or undertaking a major organisational restructuring. An organisation seeks help because there are major projects where the client does not have sufficient in-house expertise, but where once the change has been introduced, the job can be maintained internally. They know that they are getting an individual who has not only done the job before, but will have done it for a far larger enterprise, and is not looking for permanence. Three to nine months is the usual assignment period. Martin Wood, Head of PA's Interim Management Service assesses that interim managers are generally 50 per cent more experienced than the job demands. They are people who can 'hit the deck running' when they walk through the door on the first day. They are people who have visibly succeeded in corporate life, and who are often financially secure because of redundancy, early retirement or having been bought out.

● ● ● Norrie Johnston: thriving on challenge

In the past two and a half years, Norrie Johnston has worked on interim assignments for organisations as diverse as IBM, Westinghouse, IMI and the Engineering Training Authority. Each assignment has lasted no more than nine months. Each has demanded of him that he walks into difficult situations, makes a rapid analysis of what is needed, makes and sells his recommendations, starts the process of implementation and then exits. Ask him why he has taken on jobs that are fraught with complexities, and mean getting to grips rapidly with tasks, people and culture, and he says 'It's fun'. His facial expression shows he means it.

Starting life as a chemical engineer, he quickly made the shift from technical specialist, to sales and marketing. For nearly twenty years he worked with a series of major manufacturing companies in increasingly senior roles; ending his corporate career as Managing Director for Ricardo Technical Communications. He left, having returned the core business to profitability, and having made the decision that he now wanted to work independently.

His choice of interim management as a means of allowing him to continue his high need to achieve came from his own experience of having encouraged a previous employer to employ an interim manager. It would enable him to work within businesses with problems, and prepare him for his eventual goal of buying into a business and running it himself. Rather than seeing interim management as a last stage career move for the retired executive, he views it as a distinct career stage offering flexibility and the opportunity to develop his own business interests.

In his 40s, Norrie Johnston is younger than many interimers, but he shares their general profile of an experienced manager with a proven record, who in his case can offer a wide portfolio of skills in sales, marketing, strategy, planning and general management to industrial clients. The demands of the role are considerable. He has to make an impact from day one, knowing that he is both denied the transition period allowed to permanent employees and that he is under the microscope as an outsider, who is being charged out at a rate which can seem high to the client. Within two weeks he has to be on top of the brief and asking the right questions, and within four to six weeks to be ready to recommend actions. He has to work within cultures which can vary dramatically, and within which he may not feel instinctively at home. Having diagnosed the problems, he then has to be able to sell his recommendations to board members. In this sense he is no different from consultants but his involvement then extends beyond, to making it happen through the use of his managerial skills. When he leaves, it is important to him that he can keep in touch with his clients, so that he can follow up on how his input has impacted on the bottom line. That is a source of both references and professional pride.

He is helped in achieving a lot in a short period of time by the fact that he is operating as a board member, and therefore has both the backing of board members and a remit to contribute to strategic decisions. Having previously delivered on projects larger than those of the assignment, he is confidently able to predict ambitious time frames for results – and be proved right. In order to deliver, however, he has to have the backing of the client both financially and in terms of their commitment to achieving the goal. He needs clear objectives, since these will drive input and the means of evaluating his contribution.

The rewards of the career choice are earnings commensurate with his salary as a corporate executive, and the opportunity to get inside organisations he would never otherwise have seen. He averages 200 paid days a year, a target that self-employed consultants will look on with envy. He is able to do this because the role of recruitment consultancies in placing him on assignment replaces the marketing time he would need to spend in finding work as an independent. In this context, the 25–30 per cent fee they take for their work in presenting him to prospective clients is more than offset by his high utilisation rate. Where some of those seeking the periphery look for the contrast of intense working followed by time out, Norrie fills up time gaps between assignments with independent consultancy work. He has never been without an interim assignment for more than six weeks. The potential down sides of time away from home and a fragmented social life are aspects he grew familiar with during his corporate career. It also means he can totally focus on the job in hand, from Monday to Friday.

For Norrie, interim management is a means by which his career motivator of delivering results can be satisfied. He sees himself as a 'professional manager of change', who when the time is right will move out of delivering his services to clients, to delivering results for his own company. He is a successful example of interim management in action, because the needs of the employer and his own needs are matched. He doesn't seek full-time employment, and while he may sometimes hanker to stay on a little longer to find out what happens next, he also knows that with the settling in of his contribution, the job would become too small for him.

Your experience base may not yet be broad or deep enough for interim assignments, but it is still a goal which can be consciously worked towards during core organisational time.

● ● ● What's your peripheral deal?

If life on the periphery is where you believe your interests can best be met, then it's time to start considering the deal you want to create. Are you happier at the thought of operating as a contractor or a subcontractor? Are you looking to work alone or with others? Are you stimulated by the prospect of continuing your organisational career to the highest level you can achieve, and then moving out, or are you already starting to consider how you can prepare yourself for a move away from the core. Whatever your preference, fill in the dealing box.

Preferred Peripheral Role(s)				
	I expect	Potential risks or conflicts of expectation	Ways of resolving	Actions I can take now
Client will expect of me				
	I can offer	Potential mismatch of offerings	Ways of resolving	Actions I can take now
Client should offer me				

Remember

☐ The mark of a peripheral worker is that they operate as a verb rather than a noun. Peripheral working is about doing. Those who place a high value on title or professional identity will be uncomfortable with being assessed for what they do, not what they are.

☐ Self-employment is a choice for some, but an imposition for an increasing number of professional and managerial employees. Success and failure will be less shaped by lack of skills, than by failure to recognise the conditions in which an individual can operate outside of an organisational career.

☐ There is a growing amount of space at the periphery, but the deals available are shaped by the level of discontinuity an individual can tolerate, and the level of expectation they hold. Career dealers should look to contribute at the highest level that matches with their offerings.

☐ Planning for the periphery is an important skill. It requires the same attention to self-development, acquisition of market intelligence and monitoring of the environment as is demanded of those who want to stay in the core, with the added dimension that information and monitoring will be simultaneously internal and external. Even if living on the edge is a medium- or long-term goal, there are actions that can be taken now to help make it a successful move.

☐ Your present employer may become your most important client, so that managing the shift to the periphery requires you to sustain visible commitment, even while it may be organisational disenchantment which is directing the change.

☐ Operating at the edge can open up the opportunity of multiple deals that reflect a more multi-faceted perspective than was possible as an organisational careerist.

☐ If you are looking to balance your life, your options at the periphery will be limited, but if you are looking for a different rhythm to your working life, then the periphery can be an exciting place to be.

" *Self monitoring isn't self indulgence. It's the database you use for developing your strength when you look to change the deal.* **"**

take your career pulse

'If it's not fun where you're working, change it,
because that's the only reason to be there.'
Andrew Ferguson

Having established what's required of the core and periphery, a new question has to be asked, 'When do you know it's time to change?' If, as Michael Portillo has argued, 'job security will mean fewer jobs for life but more jobs in a lifetime', how do we recognise the moment when it is right for us as individuals to make a change, independent of labour market trends? How do we recognise those things about ourselves which we want to take into our future, wherever that may be. How do we capitalise on those inner themes which give us a sense of purpose and self-confidence? We start by taking our career pulse.

'You have survived the cutbacks, you know there is a job for you, so tell me what keeps you here now?' I asked a manager at a career workshop. He looked at me blankly. So focused was he on simply being there that thoughts of what he wanted from being there had gone. It's easy to continue operating at survival level, but as a long-term career strategy it's one which cannot feed into a sense of self-worth and security. There is no point agreeing continuously to learn, in response to an organisational edict, unless you know why you want to learn. Why is it that four year olds can distinguish between dinosaur species and their parents can't? It's because their interest and motivation are fully engaged. Dinosaurs form an important part of their play and imagination. What holds true for a four year old is as true for a 44 year old. You will not be able to engage fully in your part of the contract unless you are in tune with your own career

165

monitor. It's the one which tells you whether you are doing what is right for you.

● ● ● Your life shape

A first step in taking your career pulse is to look at the overall shape of your life. Each day we each have the same amount of

"A first step in taking your career pulse is to look at the overall shape of your life."

resource, twenty-four hours, to input into our lives. How we spread that resource differs greatly, depending on the demands placed on us and the amount of freedom we have in allocating that time. Consider how you alloc-

ate your twenty-four-hour input between the various demands in your life. It may look like this:

Charting input

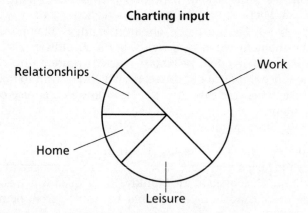

This is the time input chart of someone who gives considerable amounts of time to their work, significant time to life outside work and relationships and a relatively small amount of time to home. It could be the chart of a 25 year old or a 55 year old. Their inputs are the same, but the outputs in terms of satisfaction could be very different. To a 25 year old, with a high drive to succeed quickly, an active personal life and a view of home as a place to recover, the output satisfaction chart looks like this:

Charting satisfaction

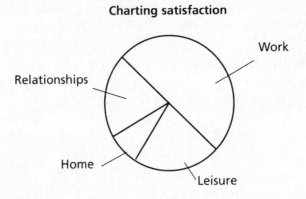

The amount of time they give to work is easily matched by the satisfaction they get from it. They might be willing to give even more time, since time maintaining domestic life is seen as unsatisfying. They are living a work hard, play hard existence which provides a satisfying return on their time investment. In contrast a colleague with ten years more experience and a family may assess the input:output ratio very differently:

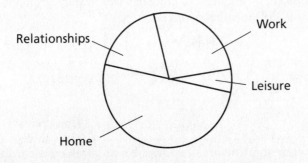

While work takes most of their time, it is not giving a satisfying return on investment. They are no longer getting the rewards which sustained motivation, or they are bored by having been in the same job for too long. Neither is leisure time as enjoyable as they would wish. The time given to building business contacts through joining local associations has become a burden. They don't enjoy the company, or find much in common with many of the people they are giving time to. In contrast, the value of home life has greatly increased – a fact that only increases frustration because time there is so limited. As a first level indicator, the 25 year old is getting sufficient return to motivate a continuation of performance and satisfaction, our 35 year old needs to take stock.

Complete the input/output charts for yourself to take a first look at whether it's time for a career check. Don't be constrained by the four categories which I have used, you may have many more roles in your life which need to be reflected in your balance sheet.

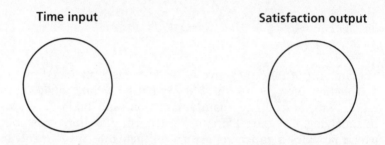

Time input   **Satisfaction output**

If work is not providing the return which you expect then it's time to ask another question. How is your skills:enjoyment ratio? Robin Linnecar of KPMG suggests to managers who attend his workshops that they need to consider where they sit against the two axis of skills and enjoyment.

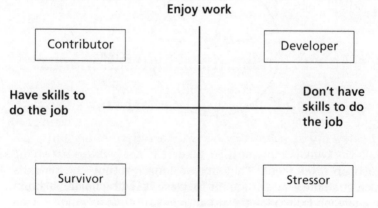

In all the focus on acquiring the skills to remain employable, there can be an unasked question – do you still want to do it?

If you enjoy the job, but don't have the skills then your motivation for development will be high. You are a **Developer**. You are looking to increase your organisational and personal value.

If you don't have the skills and don't enjoy the work, you are vulnerable, both in organisational terms and in terms of your own self-esteem. You are a **Stressor**. You are experiencing stress because of a sense of inadequacy in dealing with what is demanded of you, while the organisation will see you as failing to meet their expectations.

If you have the skills to remain employed but are no longer enjoying it, then you are operating as a **Survivor**. You can do what is required of you, but your will to contribute will be limited by your lack of satisfaction.

If you enjoy the work and have the skills required, you are equipped to cope with change and to move forward. You are both inputting into the organisation and into your own sense of satisfaction. You are a **Contributor**.

Assessing the quality of your input against the satisfaction output highlights that being able to assess our skills is not enough. Knowing that you have the skill set which is now being rewarded in the organisation's competency profiles is not in itself a motivator, unless they are related to skills which you value in yourself. If considering your skills: enjoyment ratio highlights that the balance now lies with input over output, then it's time to start monitoring your needs.

● ● ● Robert Pinder: the skilled self-monitor

Robert Pinder has had a career that has led him from his twenties to his late thirties based on acute attention to his internal self-monitor. It has led him to make decisions which to others have often seemed high risk. They have seen him as a contributor, when he has felt like a survivor and demanded more out of his work. It hasn't led to an easy working life, but it is one which, because it is personally guided, has developed in him strong career resilience.

When Robert was about to leave university he was horrified at the thought of being involved in anything so predictable as the milk round process, in which students compete for graduate posts with blue chip companies. He deliberately left with no plans, except a desire to try out interesting things. So when he saw a post for a croupier in a London casino he immediately applied with hundreds of others, and was selected. For eight months he enjoyed the vicarious glamour of watching well-known names win and lose large amounts of money. He was about to acquire the Inspector's qualification that would have enabled him to travel the world attracting high earnings, when he chose to leave. Why? Because the job lacked any intellectual stimulation. He left with no job to go to, but having made a link between his enjoyment of selling ideas to others (he is extremely personally persuasive) and marketing.

His attempts to get into marketing proved unsuccessful, but instead he was offered jobs as a salesman for a paper company, and as a media buyer for a major advertising agency. There was no contest. The sales job might pay more, but the advertising agency offered excitement. He found himself thrown in at the deep end, negotiating with TV companies to buy air time, and within weeks having to face the managing director of a leading FMCG company, who was furious at TV ratings for his company's ad. In managing to placate the client when he knew the agency was at fault, he realised once again his ability to sell ideas. After a year, he had moved from developer to contributor, and it was then that the question of personal values raised itself. To be a good buyer, he needed to believe in the products. He found that difficult to do and, more significantly, found he was more interested in observing the ways in which people around him behaved than in improving the sales of baked beans. Knowing that he was in a privileged position and occupying a role that many graduates would die for, did not enable him to hide from himself that he did not see what he was doing as useful. Once again he left with no work to move to.

Leaving allowed time for reflection on when he had felt a sense of enjoyment. He remembered the strong interest he had held in Third World issues while a student, his involvement in an international society and his travels in India. Those memories, combined with a sense of his personal skills, led him to becoming the co-ordinator for a development education centre in London; a centre funded by Oxfam, to educate people in the UK on issues affecting developing countries. He accepted a salary cut to enter a world which for three years was totally absorbing. He worked long hours, organised events, campaigned, fund raised and was sustained by working with people who stimulated him and provided close friendships. His application of skills was evident in the funds he attracted to the centre, and his enjoyment in the complete commitment he was willing to give. When internal politics led to his resignation, he once again did so with no sense of what was to follow.

What he did was to spend a year teaching in Sudan – an opportunity to put theory into practice, with no resources, often no pay and a class of 106. It was a difficult year, when both his skills and enjoyment were often challenged, but he took from it a growing sense of curiosity about how people develop. On his return he consciously compromised and accepted a job in a local authority careers service, because it gave him the financial backing to attend a career counselling diploma. The course did not stimulate him, the job even less so. Rather than sit out his time, he acknowledged the importance to him of understanding people more fully and while still completing the diploma, began a part-time Master's degree in Occupational Psychology.

This time he knew he had made the right choice and when he saw a job advert in the *Guardian* for a small consultancy seeking an occupational psychologist, he sensed it was 'his job'. They were wanting someone who was independent and could be thrown in at the deep end – Robert had shown this time and time again. Three days into the job he was running an assessment centre for a major UK organisation, loving every minute and knowing this was his big break. For three years the equation between enjoyment and learning held strong, as each week offered new challenges. The break came when he wanted a new type of learning – to be responsible for a new venture in the organisation. The owner offered him the responsibility, but would not give him a financial stake. Suddenly the equation shifted, and his internal dialogue told him, 'I am competent, I am confident, I am earning this organisation a lot of money, but what am I getting back for the overhead I am supporting.' From that point on he became unmanageable, and soon after he left to work independently.

The story could end here, but in Robert's case the timing was not right. He moved to Scotland to be with his partner, and found that while he had saleable skills, internally he had not taken on the role of independent consultant. He found it hard working from home and distracted himself through spending enormous amounts of time working on the dissertation he had not previously had time to complete. When a phone call brought a job offer to work as a researcher in a management centre, he rushed at the opportunity. Within a short time he knew he had made a mistake. He had run for safety, but when he experienced it, it did not satisfy. He was discomfitted by what he saw as a culture of complacency. When he considered whether he was prepared to learn the political rules that would help him to build his career there, he concluded he was not. Again he resigned, but this time knowing that he would not ever want to be part of an organisation again. He spent the next four months travelling in South America, returning to Oxford in a cold December with no clear sense of what would happen next.

In the early months he was twice tempted to join established consultancies, but each time he recognised his panic symptoms and stuck with his own sense of self. When he was able to say 'I don't want that job', he felt an enormous sense of relief. Even when he had no other work to do, he knew he was making the right decision. Slowly Integra Associates grew and two years on he is earning more money than he has ever earned. More importantly, he is doing work he visibly enjoys. Ask Robert why self-employment is better the second time around, and the difference lies in a sense of confidence, based not on the shelter of an organisation, but on the value of what he gives his clients. He says, 'I now earn money from who I am, and that's a great confidence builder'. He is able to concentrate his skills on what he values. He has moved beyond accepting a job in order to be able to meet his bills to being able to see himself as a specialist working with high-level teams on process issues. He is deeply committed to helping organisations change culture and to learn more effectively, through focusing on the dynamics of key organisational teams. It is work which he describes as 'exciting and frightening'.

In reviewing his career, he is very aware of the internal monitor which drives his sense of moving forward. For him to be operating as his best self, he needs to be intellectually stimulated, to be creative and to be working in new areas. He needs to have the scope for spontaneity, so that he is not working on what is already established, but is always involved in pushing things forward. He needs to be learning continuously, and to have independence of action. It is important for him that he defines how each day is going to be, and that his time is not wasted by having to interact on the basis of what is expected of him. Most of all he needs to be able to feel that his values are in alignment with those he is working with. When that sense of misalignment becomes conscious he has to move on, or he is operating in survivor mode. Being a survivor is not an option for him.

Robert Pinder is an active self-monitor, while many of those who have been living an organisational career are not. External monitoring skills may be acute, in terms of reading changes in organisational politics, business changes, sectoral influences and social shifts. They are able to direct their career efforts to match with a changing organisational agenda, but their internal monitor is an unflexed muscle. To develop that muscle and to use it as a guide requires us to review the past and to assess the present as a means of defining the future.

● ● ● What have you learnt from the past?

One way of helping you to identify those things which you need to put into your career deal is to review what has fed into past motivation. Think of a **previous** job that has given you enjoyment, and draw a line which represents your motivational moods during your time in it. It may look something like this:

Motivational Line

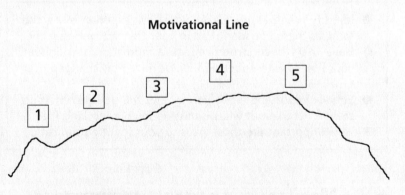

For this individual:
Peak one came when the sense of deskilling that comes with a job move was forgotten with the first assignment in which they were able to make a contribution.

173

Peak two came with a successful project in which they had a sense of ownership.

Peak three came with handling a major customer who was threatening to take away business, but was won over by their commitment to building a strong relationship.

Peak four came with being given a major account to handle and seeing it grow significantly.

Peak five came in seeing the quality of their work recognised through being asked to help out a team which was in difficulty.

These peaks are based around involvement, externally recognised success and being able to handle firefighting situations. It was these that provided the drive to work hard. When such opportunities went away enjoyment and skill went out of balance and it was time to look elsewhere.

Identify the peaks in your motivational line and recognise the things which you need if you are to operate as your best self. What themes are highlighted?

Then repeat the exercise for the job you are currently in, focusing on both the peaks and the troughs:

- Identify whether the peaks you now experience are the same as those you identified in your first motivational line.
- Have there been strong repeated motivators throughout your life, as with Robert Pinder, or have they changed over time?
- Equally important, when you look at the troughs, what do they tell you about what is missing in your working life?
- How important are those gaps to your input:output ratio?

●●● Monitor your personal environment

Focusing on what you have learnt about your personal work motivators is only one source of information. Equally important is to monitor those things which are coming into and out of your life.

Psychologist Donald Super tells us that we each occupy life space filled with all the roles that are part of us. As one role changes in the space it requires, it has implications for the others. That life space can be represented as a set of circles, the total balance of which captures our life at any moment in time.

Picturing life space

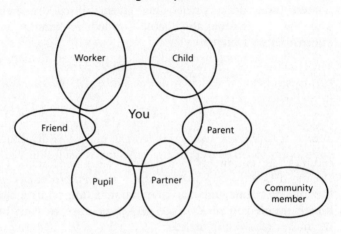

Some roles may be totally absent from our life space for a while, only to demand a major share at another time. The individual who left school determined never to study again can be the same person who in mid-years gives up large amounts of life space in order to return to study. The child who gained early independence from its parents finds in later life that they take on parenting their parents, at a point where they thought they were freeing up life space from parenting their children. The individual who has dominated their life space with work discovers, when work is no longer so satisfying, that they do not know how to fill the hole left in their life space. It is important regularly to assess our life space in order to recognise where there is a need to rebalance roles, and where that balance may come from.

● ● ● Barney Tremblay: a life space shifter

Barney Tremblay is now Director of Crawford Tremblay, a leading consultancy specialising in personal image and confidence skills. She is an outgoing American, a graduate in communications and psychology, who in her early career years devoted a good deal of her life space to establishing herself as a TV and radio presenter. When she came to the UK in 1980, as wife of a rising airline executive, her space became dominated by the roles of executive wife and mother. She saw herself having a distinct role in supporting the career of her husband. At the time she was happy with the balance of her life. She was a skilled hostess who accompanied her husband on business trips, knowing her personality skills added a dimension to his successful performance.

The balance of her space was altered by four events, the connectiveness of which was not visible at the time. The move from boom into recession meant that the role of executive wife was no longer required. Accompanying spouse on business trips became a corporate overhead to be cut, so that her opportunities to contribute declined. This not only took away a role, it also reduced the amount of time spent with a workaholic husband. During a holiday trip to Fiji, she was unexpectedly exposed to the idea of colour analysis. The potential importance of the idea hit her immediately. As a TV presenter she had been aware of the power of makeup artists and wardrobe to affect her mood for the day. On a good day they provided the 'psychological warfare' to help her deal with whatever came her way. Through a chance encounter, she relearnt that colour was something that affects people's lives. When the trip moved on to Australia, she bought every book she could find on image and the psychology of colour. For a year she was an avid student – but one without a purpose. She had no goal in mind, she had simply found a subject that aroused her interest.

When the unwillingness of her husband to create more life space for his wife and family led to separation, the need to create a work role came into immediate focus. At this point the connection between colour and earning a living was made. She attended a training course to qualify as an image consultant and it quickly became evident that she knew more than the trainer. Her university education as a psychologist enabled her to see that image consultancy was providing right answers, but without acknowledging or understanding the importance of individual differences. At a time when the industry was focused on seeing image consultancy as a product to be sold to groups of women; a 1980s replacement for the Tupperware party, she knew there was more it could offer. She saw a market in the corporate world, where it could be directly linked to issues of self-presentation and effectiveness.

Growing her work life space was not painfree She quickly became aware that while she had been confident in using her skills to promote her husband, she had lost confidence in applying them to herself. Her confidence grew initially through working with women in a domestic environment, but her work space expanded once more when she heard Pauline Crawford speak. She recognised a fellow spirit and told Pauline, much to her surprise, that they were going to work together. The opportunity did not come for two years, by which time both were ready to move the business into new areas, built on the development of confidence skills and business behaviour.

For Barney, the monitoring process was not just making a necessary shift in role sizes in response to her divorce. It was recognising that moment when something important came into view and storing it away until the time came to act on the awareness.

● ● ● Map out your life space

If you think about your own life space, how is it currently occupied? Map out the relative sizes of your role demands and recognise where there have been changes. In considering the changes look for where shifts create new demands or new opportunities. If circumstances have increased the amount of life space demanded by work, then the need may be to focus on increasing the personal value of that work space, so that survival does not consume all your energies. If roles of parent or partner are becoming less demanding, is there new energy to redirect towards new roles? Or are the roles becoming so overwhelming that negotiation for change is a necessity? If one role is all encompassing, then consider the impact to your self-esteem if that role was taken away, and recognise the need to use some of that energy in building up other roles.

● ● ● Recognise what is coming into view

When Barney Tremblay heard her first seminar on colour, she had no idea of the importance it would come to play in her life.

She only recognised that it struck some chord within her. She acted on that recognition through opening up to the idea of learning. Being able to recognise those indicators is an important part of self-monitoring. When we recognise them it helps to prepare us for the transition of making a shift in our life space balance. If we fail to recognise them, we can miss opportunities for moving forward.

Consider ...

● What sort of people do you now enjoy spending time with – has that changed in recent time?

● What types of books attract you when you go book browsing – are there any patterns, and are they different from five years ago?

● What are the things which you choose to do in your job, and has that changed in the last two years?

● What gives you most enjoyment in your working life, and has that changed in the last two years?

● What are the things that you want to learn about, as distinct from having to learn about?

Self-monitoring isn't self-indulgence. It's the database you use for developing your strength when you look to change the deal. As I was writing this chapter, a journalist phoned and quizzed me at length. The conversation became more and more irritable, as I tried to explain why I believed dealing was the only way to view career management, and he professed that the idea was incomprehensible. Finally, after thirty minutes of non-communication, I asked him, 'What is it that makes it so difficult for you to accept?' 'Well,' he said, 'I worked for a national newspaper for thirty years, and I cannot imagine how I could have gone into the editor's office and negotiated a different deal. I wouldn't have known where to start.' 'You could', I replied, 'If you had had a strong sense of what you needed and why you needed it. But if you only monitored yourself against what they asked of you, you are right, your basis for dealing was weak.'

Remember

☐ We each have an internal measure by which we measure our pay-off in terms of satisfaction gained from the input we are giving our work. If the satisfaction output is out of balance, then our motivation and desire to contribute will decline.

☐ We need to plot our position along the two axes of skills competence and work enjoyment. To ignore either makes us vulnerable to the ending of our employment contract and the decline of our self-esteem.

☐ By plotting our motivation over the periods of time we have spent in jobs, we can build up a profile of those things we need to sustain motivation. They are powerful career guides, if we learn to trust in them.

☐ All of us have a mosaic of roles which fill up our life space. We need to monitor their shifts, because change can both create demands and open up new living space.

☐ When we monitor ourselves we must also monitor our response to those things that come into our environment, and recognise things of value which pass before us. It is by receiving those gifts that we can open up new possibilities which make the negotiation of a new deal easier.

" *New beginnings don't come waving flags, they tend to come in images, feelings and indicators which invite us to find out more.* **"**

make the transition

The last chapter seemed to suggest that you can negotiate a new career deal once you know you are unhappy with what you have. As though knowing what you do want will flow seamlessly from knowing what you don't. Experience tells me it's not like that. The sense of unhappiness with what we have can be acute, without having any sense of what we would like in its place. That immediately throws us back into a closed loop. For many of us our only career model has been to discover what we are good at, find an opportunity that matches, and polish our job search skills. Then to discover ten or twenty years on that we don't like what we have, but can't verbalise what we want, throws us into confusion, or into attempts to rationalise our situation:

● Maybe no one really knows what they want.

● At least I have got a job.

● I'll just have to learn to live with it, and do what I enjoy doing when I retire (on the assumption that you can't do what you enjoy while you are working).

The idea that career planning starts with knowing our goal and ends with achieving it is a powerful but erroneous one. It explains why many of the early career interviews I had with clients would end with their apologising for not knowing what they wanted, and my sense of inadequacy at not having got them any nearer to knowing their goal. We were both caught up in goals, when we should have been focusing on **transitions**.

● ● ● The transition process

A transition is a passage from one state to another, a recognition that something has ended but that the future and one's place within it are not yet established. My clients were in transit, when they were eager to reach their new destination. What they carried was a strong sense that what had been was no longer enough. They had left the old station, but were so uncomfortable with this recognition that they sought, as quickly as possible, to find a new beginning. As a supposed helper, I sensed their unease and wanted to make it right for them as quickly as possible. In reality, the new beginning could only come after an often painful period of living with uncertainty.

It's because moving is so uncomfortable that for many people the instinct is to deny the ending. When the redundancy notice arrives, the formal ending is clear, but stories of employees who pretend to friends that they are still employed are vivid illustrations of self-denial. For others, less dramatic signals about an ending are being given out, but are not received, for fear of the void that will follow. Signals that the time to end the present deal has come are emitted in four processes:

- **Connection** ties loosen. To the outside world you may look as though you are still doing a good job, but your sense of involvement is diminishing. The desire to make more of what you have is replaced by a grudging acceptance of doing no more than you have to do.

- **Contracting** no longer satisfies. Once the contract was a pair of scales in which your input was placed on one side and the organisation's offers created balance. Now the organisational offers weigh unevenly against your needs.

- **Charm** disappears. Activities that you were happy to engage in and people you enjoyed being with no longer satisfy. There is a sense of disenchantment, where you ask questions such as, 'Why am I doing something which seems pointless to me?', or 'How can I spend time with people, who look at the world so differently?'

- **Compass** direction is lost. There is a sense of disorientation, of not knowing what to do, but having a clear sense that what you are doing isn't what you are meant to be doing.

It is not necessary to experience all four processes, any one can be enough to signal that it's time to renegotiate or exit. For women, a clear ending is often childbirth and finding on return from maternity leave that conventional career rewards hold less appeal. For others it's the questioning of the importance of what they are doing which is their clearest signal. People can spend large parts of their career with these feelings unspoken, for fear of their consequences. They are explained away as indulgences which are not allowable in a mature adult with financial responsibilities. Yet any person who makes the break, who announces that they are leaving or going off in an entirely new direction, finds they are an immediate magnet for confessions from others around them. They are harbouring similar feelings but cannot see a way out. The courage of one person in stating they want a different career deal translates itself into an 'outing' process where others see the changer as acting for them by proxy.

●●● Understanding endings

The beginning of a new deal starts with acknowledging the ending of the old one. This acknowledgement can take a long time. For Nick Orosz, of whom we hear more later, it took twelve years before he could accept that ending was the only way of making a new beginning. He is typical of many for whom letting go of a rope is an inch-by-inch process. For others, such as Robert Pinder, dramatic endings are the norm. They need immediately to get on to the new and will run away from the old, even if they have no sense of what they are running towards. Neither approach is right or wrong – just as some people end a telephone conversation the minute business is done, and others need to linger and wind down the conversation before they can put the receiver down. Each of us needs to recognise both our own pattern of endings, and where we are in the polarities which mark the move from entry to exit. Ask yourself where in the continuum are you between:

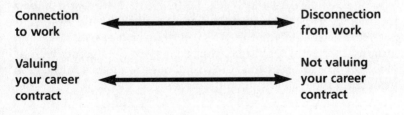

| Connection to work | ←——————→ | Disconnection from work |
| Valuing your career contract | ←——————→ | Not valuing your career contract |

| Charmed | | Questioning |
| by what you do | ←————————→ | of what you do |

Sure of your		Unsure of your
compass	←————————→	compass
direction		direction

Even if your readings tell you the conditions are right for ending your present career deal, this gives you no clue as to when. Each of us has an internal model of how we manage endings, whether in work, friendships, or partnerships. Past experiences will tell you whether you are someone who:

● finds it difficult to recognise when a relationship has run its course and attempts to suppress the recognition, or is someone who has to move on as soon as the awareness is made.
● finds it easier to stick with something even if it is uncomfortable, than to move on to something new.
● would rather be the first to leave a social event or the last.
● feels excitement or anxiety at the thought of something new.

Recognising our pattern of endings is important to understanding why you may have done little to change a situation at work which you know with your intelligence is no longer right for you. For the moment, simply acknowledging that you are in the process of ending may be enough.

Entering the discomfort zone

Ending is the start of beginning, but in the middle is an uncomfortable period – the **discomfort zone**. This recognition of the necessity of both ending and a period of confusion as a prelude to new beginnings is a knowledge that is shared across cultures and religions. I am writing this on Good Friday, a day which in Christian religion marks the ending of the life of Jesus Christ. It is followed by Easter Saturday, a day in which the fate of Jesus is uncertain, before Easter Sunday when resurrection shows his followers that their faith has a future and a new beginning. This cycle, whether seen as having a literal or a symbolic truth, is found in other religions and in tribal cultures around the world. The tribe, that sends away its young men at adolescence, in order that their readiness to enter adulthood is tested by their elders, literally marks the rite of passage into adulthood with physical markings to the body. They can then re-enter the tribe with a new status and role, which is clearly visible.

In many stories of Greek legend the same pattern is repeated: a dramatic event, which marks the end of stability, a period of great uncertainty, of being cast adrift, and finally after much pain, the finding of a new way, which could not have been predicted at the start. It's a theme so often repeated that it clearly offers a universal truth and yet, because of pain and the fear of pain, we try to avoid recognising it. Instead people choose to stay with the pain of what they have. Andrew Ferguson, founder of Breakthrough, an organisation which supports individuals in achieving both self-employment and personal growth, believes 'The discomfort of undergoing change is nothing compared to the pain of resisting it'.

We fight against going into the discomfort zone because it doesn't fit with a model of life which says, 'Know what you want and go for it'. Entering the zone is an admission that we don't know what we want, and we don't know how we may emerge. What we may also fear is that what results will be incompatible with what we have come to expect:

● I can't consider any other options because I have to earn a good salary.

● I can't afford to change my life because of what it might mean for my family.

● I can't give up a role I've worked hard for because what would I then be.

Can't usually means won't. Won't is why, even when an ending is made visible in the act of redundancy, outplacement counsellors tell me the chief aim of many clients is not to define a new beginning but to reinstate the old as quickly as possible. They deny that it is the ending of an old career contract that has caused them to lose their jobs, and look to find a haven where the old is still in place. When redundancy comes again, as statistically it is likely to do, they are no better equipped to deal with it the second time, because they never allowed themselves to acknowledge the need for a new beginning. They are like rock stars who several years into a relationship, when the attraction of passion wanes, trade in one partner for an indistinguishable but younger version. It's an easier option than acknowledging one ending and working through how the next stage of the relationship could be.

●●● The transition curve

The discomfort zone is a hard place to be. William Bridges calls it a 'time of lostness and emptiness before life resumes an intelligible pattern and direction'. It's part of the process which Elizabeth Kubler Ross first identified in the late 1960s in her work with terminally ill patients. She found their first reaction was often to deny the fact, to block out the news they had been given and to carry on as if nothing had changed. This was frequently followed by anger, the understandable rage of 'Why me?', or attempts to bargain with their fate. A period of confusion, uncertainty and depression followed before an acceptance of the ending of life brought with it a sense of peace. Not all patients followed this cycle, some never moved beyond denial or anger, or were unable to find a way out of the uncertainty, but for those who did, dying came to have its own meaning.

The same pattern has been found in situations as diverse as the grieving process and movement into a new job. It was visible in the career attitudes of long-serving managers, whom I surveyed in the insurance industry. There were those who denied that anything had changed, despite the fact that colleagues around them had lost their jobs. There were others who felt angry at the organisation for breaking its career promises. Some wanted to bargain, by promising to do whatever was necessary as long as they could still be promoted, and there were others who could accept the ending and were willing to have a different career future. Some were totally confused and simultaneously held beliefs in opposition to each other. On the one hand they could see that promotion was not possible, and that not to be promoted wasn't the end of the world. On the other, what they wanted more than anything else was promotion. They were firmly stuck in the discomfort zone.

Getting through the discomfort zone

So how to get through the discomfort zone, when you can have no sense of what will be the end result? The following actions have helped those who have worked through the process and found a new beginning:

● **Accept** that discomfort is a sign that something is happening internally. It might not be visible to anyone else, but the unease is acknowledgement that you are wanting to move on.
● **Don't try to rush** through it by reacting. The temptation is to grab at any opportunity that presents itself. A friend rings up with news of a job opportunity, and you rush at it, thinking it's got to be better than this. It mightn't be – it may simply offer the career contract equivalent of the rock star marriage.
● **Talk.** It's no accident that personal growth groups are full of people working through transitions. At their best they work to help clarify what it is you are saying to yourself, and give support in allowing people to say and think the unthinkable. You might not need a formal group, but you do need people who can listen to you without telling you how you should be.
● **Forget goals.** This may seem like madness. Surely the point of transition is to get to the new goal as quickly as possible. No. The point of transition is to clear the space so that a new beginning can come in. When it does, time and time again, it comes in an unexpected way. It is true development, in the literal sense of an unfolding. Those who have found a new way rarely see it as coming with a bang, with a sudden flash of inspiration. Instead they speak of gradually becoming aware of 'indications'; of finding themselves being attracted to something, and once they respond to that sense, opportunities to act on it arise. It bears little resemblance to the 'Aha!' career matching model they have carried with them from adolescence. It is much more tentative, and impressionistic.

The period of transition is one of realigning what you thought you were with what you now are. Inevitably, it is a time of push and pull. One day you will feel certain that you are ready for change, the next all the sound reasons why you shouldn't, can't, mustn't will rear their heads. A glimpse into an exciting future is immediately clouded by a sense of depression about everything that would be unsettled by the change. The emergence is as unclear, and tentative as the entry, but gradually possibilities will start to show themselves. Just as plants lose their leaves in autumn, lie dormant in winter and then miraculously bud in spring, the end of a transition will be marked by opportunities to grow new buds. They won't all appear at once, but their visibility is a signal to you and others that you are renewing. If it seems difficult to allow yourself the possibility of accepting ending, transition and a new career beginning, then follow Nick Orosz's story, because he was once like you.

● ● ● Nick Orosz: a career made through transition

Nick Orosz represented career success in the 1980s. A Cambridge law graduate, he was recruited by a leading City law firm, had a spectacularly successful career as a corporate lawyer, earned large amounts of money and yet knew almost from day one that he was misplaced. He took twelve years to allow himself this recognition and, in the painful process of finding what he really wanted to do, also discovered that the lawyer in him which he had seen as a stranglehold on his true ambitions, was an important part of him that simply needed to find its place.

When Nick left Cambridge, he took time out to travel in India and South East Asia. For him it was a 'life-changing experience', which has shaped his subsequent deep interest in Buddhism and Tibet. He spent a month at a Tibetan monastery and, perhaps not surprisingly, found the transition into working in the City difficult. He quickly discovered that the best way of protecting his individuality and difference was to hide it. He didn't speak of holidays when he went on meditation retreats. He didn't speak of the creative writing courses he attended or his love of photography, because to do so would have been seen as an implied lack of career commitment. Instead, for twelve years he knuckled down. He may have felt that he was an outsider, but he wouldn't deny that there were parts of the job he found exhilarating. He looked the part, he was seen as doing a good job, and while he could see that he lacked the ice cold determination of some of his colleagues, he shared their ambition for partner status. He worked the same long hours, he was involved in major projects dealing with company mergers and the privatisation of utilities. He was living a 'macho' City life. To him, however, it primarily meant access to an income which would allow him to retire at forty to do the things which he would rather be doing. Large amounts of time were spent in drawing up financial plans that would allow for an early release, and he used his high salary to travel. It did not escape his notice, however, that those who earned partner status, rather than easing off as a reward for previous efforts, worked harder than ever in order to justify their high rewards.

After six years, including a stint in Paris, he left to join a smaller practice, but his hopes of a shorter working week proved foundless. Seventy hours continued to be the norm. He found his health suffering and soon plans to retire at forty started to telescope. He knew he had to escape sooner. Law had become the enemy. When he tried to think of alternatives, his thoughts would lead him to legal work for charities such as Greenpeace, but financial anxiety would quickly suppress the thought. For years Nick wavered between recognising the need to end this career and fear of doing so. Money made his life bearable, and money made an escape route unthinkable. Ironically, to him, those with less earning power had more choices, because they were less trapped by material manacles.

His first glimpse of the possibility of change came with personal growth workshops. The pressures of both his working life, and his resistance to it led to the collapse of his marriage. During this time he attended workshops run by the Actor's Institute. In one designed to help those who were looking for more creativity and energy in their lives, he found the beginnings of the strength to take responsibility for himself and his life. He was introduced to the idea that it was possible to make money out of what he loved doing, whereas money was his reward for the dis-ease of doing something he disliked. What he knew he loved doing was photography, and the course encouraged him to set up a photographic exhibition where he received positive feedback and sold work. More importantly, it gave him the courage to stand up at the end of the programme and publicly announce on the 27 March 1992 that, 'Twelve months from today, I will have given up being a full-time solicitor'. He made the statement with no sense of what he would be doing, but as a positive marker that he had come to an ending. The importance was in the words. He was no longer trying and failing not to be a solicitor. He had publicly declared his intention within a clear time frame. His vision went no further than that.

Within a short period of announcing his intention, a conversation with a legal recruitment firm introduced him to the possibility of acting as an information service to a large legal practice. Conventionally it was seen as a job for a woman returner. He saw it as the perfect job for a person in transition. It only required a 35-hour week. After the high pressure, high demands of his previous life he saw it as a 'cushy job', and yet it still attracted a high salary that allowed him to support the lifestyle he was used to. He had taken the first step towards loosening the ties of a solicitor identity. His announcement of the decision to leave legal practice brought behind the door confessions of envy from colleagues whom he had previously assumed were fully committed to their careers. Instead he discovered they felt as trapped as he had, but saw no escape route.

The two years in transition gave him the out-of-work hours previously denied to explore other interests. He spent time travelling in America and took landscape photographs. He gave more time to his commitment to Tibet, and from it came an important 'indicator' for his future. In all the years when he had questioned, 'Why am I giving so much time to doing things I don't care about?', he had assumed that the lawyer was a dysfunctional part of him, even though friends told him that there was a reason why he had chosen to be a lawyer. Now, with time to spare, he became involved in setting up a conference of international lawyers to explore the rights of self-determination of the Tibetan people. The conference attracted world experts, and while acting as rappoteur for the conference proceedings he had a strong sense that his life would never be the same again. He edited a book based on the conference papers, and in doing so discovered he was using his legal skills and training on behalf of something he cared passionately about. Suddenly he had a vision of how as a lawyer he was meant to be, and it did not involve earning large amounts of money. Instead he saw himself as an expert, helping disenfranchised peoples to claim their rights. For him, this was one of the few real turning points in his life. Editing the book took large amounts of his spare time and left him exhausted, but the moment when he presented a copy to the Dalai Lama he rates as one of the highlights of his life.

If he wanted further proof of transition as a moving away from what has been, the book provided it. It was reported on in the legal press, but was regarded as an embarrassment by his employers, and a clear explanation as to why his involvement in information provision was less than total. As a consequence of the conference, however, he was invited to become a legal trustee for a number of charities, was offered a full-time job as a human rights lawyer (which he turned down), and was approached to become a part-time research fellow in international law at Cambridge University.

The transition was providing two pieces of his future career deal:

● **Creativity** – photography was becoming a hobby which could pay its way.
● **Contribution** – Tibet was emerging as an important focus for his legal skill, and was providing a sense of his career destiny.

Neither, however, promised to provide an income commensurate with his past. The third piece of his portfolio emerged directly from his desire still to live well. He consciously explored ways in which he could earn a high income from self-employment. His answer came in network marketing: the building up of a network of sales staff from whose work he could earn commission. A means by which he could passively earn money while doing other things. He had explored the idea some years ago, but had not been convinced by the products on offer. Now in a telephone call from the USA (another indicator), he was introduced to a range of healing products based on aloe vera. Because of his strong interest in natural healing, the product made a connection with him, and he was able to commit.

The two years that he gave to the transition were fully employed in putting each of the pieces in place. It was a time of hard work and, as Nick admits, it was often a painful process. The ideas which eventually emerged were three of many he tested out and this often resulted in feelings of confusion. There were few big moments of realisation, and lots of stops and starts. There were understandable fears of starvation, of watching with envy friends who had stayed on a 'proper' career ladder, and doubts that maybe he had got it all wrong and that he would wake up to find he had made a big mistake. The transition was a testing time, organically building on those things which came into his vision once he had cleared space, but also demanding of him a commitment to act.

For Nick, the important thing is 'doing it, not sitting around moping and thinking of doing it'. When his first exhibition at the

Actor's Institute led to a friend suggesting he should put up the exhibition in a cafe in a distant part of London, his first instinct was to say 'No'. Instead he said 'Yes', and the chance visit of a photographic journalist to the cafe led to magazine articles and corporate sales of his work. Similarly, accepting the transition job was a positive move in taking what was absolutely right for the short term, but would have been absolutely wrong for the long term. Involvement in the Tibetan conference was made with no sense of what it could lead to, beyond knowing it was an important part of his identity.

In November 1994 he finally left full-time work. He had set himself a financial target for what he would need to be earning from network marketing before he could let go of the security of full-time employment. Just as setting a retirement date of forty proved untenable, so Nick abandoned the financial goal and left when the time felt right. When the moment came it didn't seem like stepping over a precipice, but a guided step forward. In the months that have followed he has been proved right. His income has steadily increased, even while he was travelling in India. He has time to do the things which he values, and the lawyer in him has found its correct life space.

Nick's story is one where a transactional career deal of high earnings as compensation for high misery has been replaced with a deal based on earning money to allow space for the parts of himself which he values. He does not see his purpose as selling aloe vera, but he recognises that his purpose as a lawyer may only be achievable through doing other things, and that his creative self also has a place in his work. It is a new beginning that could only have been defined and made comfortable by living through transition.

● ● ● Are you in transit or transition?

If you can recognise that you are at an ending, then you need to take a step forward, even though that step may in the short term take you into confusion. Use the information you have collected about yourself in previous chapters to take a step away from where you are currently standing.

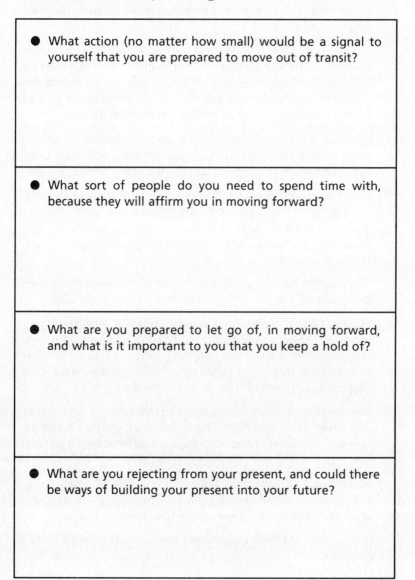

● What action (no matter how small) would be a signal to yourself that you are prepared to move out of transit?

● What sort of people do you need to spend time with, because they will affirm you in moving forward?

● What are you prepared to let go of, in moving forward, and what is it important to you that you keep a hold of?

● What are you rejecting from your present, and could there be ways of building your present into your future?

Remember

☐ Career goals do not spring fully formed, they emerge from a process of confusion, once an acceptance of an ending is made.

☐ Transition from one career deal to another cannot be hurried; it requires acceptance of ending, a willingness to live in the discomfort zone, and a commitment to acting on new beginnings.

☐ Endings can take a long time to come into our conscious awareness, because of fear of what might follow, but clues lie in our sense of disconnection with our work, our sense that the contract feels unbalanced, our disillusionment with the why of what we do and a sense of having lost our direction.

☐ When we enter the discomfort zone, we need to take care of ourselves, and to look for means of support which will allow us to live with the unease, and not bolt for the safety of the familiar.

☐ New beginnings don't come waving flags, they tend to come in images, feelings and indicators which invite us to find out more. This means you will use up lots of energy in the transition following false trails before your individual pattern will emerge.

☐ There won't be one good match that makes everything fine, there will be a best match. A deal that can be lived with.

☐ Moving out of transition is as important as moving in. It's important to recognise moments when it is important to act, and stop rehearsing. The moment when it's time to stop worrying about getting your cv perfect or your business card designed, and instead start to do business

☐ New beginnings do not have to mean the outright rejection of what has gone before. It can mean that in the process of renewal, the familiar comes to occupy a different space in your life, but one where it sits more comfortably.

☐ Moving out of transition means taking lots of small steps, which can seem dull and far removed from the glamour of the goal. Without them, however, the goal remains a dream.

☐ Moving into the new beginning means speaking of yourself as you want to be, not defining yourself by what you were.

"We need the recognition of others, but we must start with a recognition of ourselves, since we are the only certain traveller on our career journey."

build your inner core

'No one ever said on their death bed, I wish I'd worked more.'
Anonymous.

Do you remember the 'feel good' factor? Like a company perk that's removed, we never really appreciated it until it was gone. Refinding it, commentators claim, would be a true measure of recovery. Despite government figures, which show that against all usual indicators the economy is back on track, there is a resistance to accepting economic facts that is acted out in cautious spending and record saving patterns. The reasons for that resistance are multiple:

- We have seen that recovery can no longer be equated with full-employment. Can we feel good about the continued prospect of mass unemployment and the social ills that accompany it?

- We have realised that economic cycles are getting shorter and shorter, so that even while we are living through one downturn, we have memories of the previous one. How can we feel good, if we have escaped this downturn, when, on age grounds alone, the next downturn will make us more vulnerable?

- We have seen that turning round the bottom line has been inextricably linked with reducing head count, and promotion opportunities. The usual 'feel good' rewards are now increasingly difficult to obtain.

- We have realised that making long-term investments is difficult because of the difficulty of foreseeing our own future long term.

- We have recognised that 'feel good' was based on faulty

premises. Those high annual salary increases meant less about our abilities than we concluded at the time. We thought they would carry on indefinitely as a mirror of our worth – when they stopped does it mean our abilities are any the less? We thought we were the generation who would get rich through property. Now that houses are homes, not quick return investments, have we failed?

As much as politicians may want to give us a 'feel good' factor, they know that it cannot be delivered without returning the economy to the hot house of the 1980s. This leaves them with election difficulties, but it leaves us with the possibility of developing 'feel good' from a different source – ourselves. For the future, feeling good is going to come from having created an internal sense of security. Since we cannot look to the external environment to give sustainable warm feelings, the career contracting process has to include a new contracting element – that of contracting with ourselves, to provide the conditions in which we can 'feel good'. That might not equate with feel rich or feel important, but it will equate with feeling a sense of our own power.

"For the future, feeling good is going to come from having created an internal sense of security."

● ● ● Developing your own sense of power

In the past others knew who we were by our names; the present day Bakers, Taylors, Coopers and Butchers are all testimonies to their forefathers' occupations, just as the Williamsons, Johnsons and Petersons were once easily identified within their communities. Those names were markers of their position within their village, and the relative power that accrued to them. As our communities became bigger and craftsmen lost their power, those labels lost their original meaning. Instead, much of our power signalling shifted to within the workplace. Managing and leading within organisations has become related to two sources of power – the power of the position and the power of the person, with hierarchical structures often placing more importance on the former than the latter. Managers have been able to value themselves from the power given them by virtue of their job title and its ranking within the structure; their power to reward and coerce and their power to control information. Take away those sources through redundancy or new ways of working in delay-ered organisations and many individuals feel denuded of power. How can they 'feel good' when those things that bolstered them are no longer theirs.

It's not easy to imagine making the switch from core employee to self-employed contractor, consultant or interim manager, if the muscles of personal power, expertise, and persuasiveness, have been unexercised. Even those who have had a sense of their personal power, based upon their expertise as a professional, can find it shaken when they move outside. Their power as expert has often been contingent on operating in a context which provides clear messages that what they offer is valued by the organisation. Ask them to sell their expertise to a sceptical client, and their sense of personal power visibly shrinks.

● ● ● Finding the inner core

How can an individual hold on to a sense of personal power, when the organisation apparently no longer values their expertise? How can an individual develop a sense of personal power when the source of their position power is taken away? The answer has to lie in harnessing a new source of power – that of one's inner core. It's what Patricia Cleghorn, Principal of the Self Esteem Company, calls the 'inner cv': the self-esteem and confidence which enables people to deal with uncertainty. Her work is in encouraging organisations to pay attention to helping employees develop that inner cv while they are employed, in order that they feel valued by the organisation, sustain their commitment and feel able to contribute creatively. If the inner cv is a legitimate source of development while employed within the core, then it's even more crucial for those who move outside. Without it, the individual risks being tossed by the demands of whoever is offering work. A move made in order to obtain greater personal freedom becomes undermined by a sense of being trapped by the conflicting demands of clients. In the rush to please, and earn, the sense of a whole self is lost. Talk of inner wholeness may sound too much like 'New Age' philosophies for your comfort, but there are sound practical reasons for paying attention to that inner core. Those operating outside organisations quickly find that customers can be very different in their values and interests. They may be buying your personal expertise, but the use they want to make of it jars with your own values. Or an organisational employee may find themselves swamped in trying to balance their organisational values with those of a key customer or partner. Without a sense of self, the value of your own beliefs and your boundaries, the knowledge and expertise on which you are building your self-confidence, can quickly become eroded by the uses to which others want to put your skills. Being able to say 'No', is an important part of building your inner core.

Your personal career contract

As much as your career is a series of negotiated contracts over the course of your working life, **your career is also an ongoing contract with your self**.

Maintaining the value of that personal contract means asking: **Is this career decision affirming or destructive of the person who I am and want to be?**

Consider:

- How much of your confidence in your work role is based on the position of power that is given to you? Take away the certainties that come with that position, and how confident are you that you could deliver required performance?

- How much of your confidence in your work role is based on your personal power? How far are you dependent on one source of personal power – expertise, persuasiveness, or the willingness of others to accord you power, because of your personal attributes? If you were to work outside the core, what other sources of personal power would you need to develop?

- How well developed is your inner core – your sense of self, which can weather the ups and downs of working life, without feeling that the essential you is being eroded?

- How often do you take career decisions on the basis of whether they affirm the person that you want to be?

- Have you ever considered that your career contract is as much with yourself as with an employer? What are you offering and expecting of yourself – now?

How can you develop a sense of your inner core?

The key to developing a sense of your inner core is to recognise that without it there is a lack of balance. As the story of Nick Orosz illustrated, career success without meaning is unsustainable without considerable cost to the self. As the story of Gillian Edwards later in this chapter shows, without a context of meaning, it is not possible to frame career success outside of a traditional model which may be unattainable. It is only through finding our meaning that we can create a balancing weight. The two in balance rest on the fulcrum of career renewal.

American psychologist, Mark Guterman, calls this relationship one of 'generative balance'. Balance as the basis of regeneration is a daily acted out theme of nature. It is evident in areas as diverse as physics, Chinese medicine and our own physiological systems. The failure of one part of any system has consequences for the rest. We know when our bodies are out of balance, and look to put it right, and yet we often choose to ignore when our external and internal careers are out of balance. For those for whom accessing career success has been easy, the need to explore meaning has often been subverted – on the basis that success and meaning must be intertwined. It is only when career success is elusive, or it's inadequacy becomes self-evident, that the search for meaning becomes conscious. Transitions are a conscious time of searching for meaning when the scales tip heavily and old career successes become lightweight and literally 'up in the air'. It is only when that meaning is found that the two come back into balance and it is possible to move forward. To use Guterman's model:

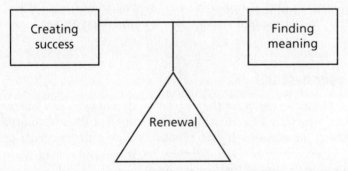

Just as balance is a key to negotiating a satisfactory psychological contract with an employer, so the balance of your internal need for meaning and its externalisation in the career success you seek are key to managing a career as a series of renewals.

● ● ● Finding the meaning of your inner core

Finding meaning does not have to imply upheaval. It does not necessarily mean the discovery that everything that has gone before has been a chimera. It can act to confirm that previous career choices have been appropriate, or to allow for realising options that previously have been blocked out. Finding meaning is as much about discovering the touchstone which gives you strength to work with uncertainties, as it is about looking for large life changes. It is because the need for meaning is so often submerged, that it is only recognised when it erupts forcibly, creating havoc in its wake. Gauguin abandoning his life as a stockbroker to become a painter in the South Pacific, Stephen Fry fleeing the London stage, Lynne Franks leaving her highly successful PR agency, are all dramatic change points – but it doesn't have to be like that. Provided we have choices beyond those of mere economic survival, we all seek to find a way of life that is true to our nature – it's just that in the focus on doing we can forget the importance of being.

> **"Finding meaning does not have to imply upheaval."**

> **"in the focus on doing we can forget the importance of being."**

Find your best self

Robert Pinder's search for the way he needed to be was a journey towards integrating his doing and his being, yet the information he needed about himself was readily available to him from his early career choices. The process of integration was about accepting the value of that knowledge.

● ● ● Integrate your doing and your being

If you have not previously thought about the integration of your doing and being as the basis for finding meaning, take some time to identify at least three times when you have had a sense of achievement. The sense could have come in any area of your life and since no one else will see your list they do not have to be achievements by anyone else's criteria. These are not for use on your public cv.

-
-
-

For one client her list looked completely unconnected:

- The time she gave a talk before 300 people just days into a completely new job.

- Running a half marathon and coming in 350th.

- Travelling alone around South East Asia.

While they seemed random, when we discussed them some recurring themes occurred:

- The need to take on things which she didn't think she could do initially.

- A lack of sense of competition with others but a strong need to compete with and push herself.

- An enjoyment of herself as a communicator.

- A recognition that as much as she liked working with others, her best sense of self came through things she did alone.

Having listed your achievements, probe them for the meaning they hold for you. Are there any patterns which give you clues as to how you need to be, in order for career success to have meaning?

Once you have recognised your 'being needs', recognise what you don't need to be, by asking yourself, 'When have I been in the wrong place?' Think of times when your senses have told you that this is not where you are meant to be.

For my client, this was more difficult, because her instincts were to see herself as deficient against the situation, rather than that the situation was not part of her being. Eventually she recognised:

● When she joined a major retail organisation, and found she could not share the values and enthusiasms of her managerial colleagues.

● When she found that the annual obsession with obtaining bonus at whatever cost, left her untouched and unmotivated, unless she had seen the year as a personally satisfying one.

● When she found that her colleagues in an insurance company saw claims only in financial terms, when she saw them in personal terms.

It was through recognising where she was not meant to be, that she came to accept that her future did not lie with an organisation. In trying to be like those around her she expended large amounts of emotional energy that were better directed in energising commitment to creating her own work.

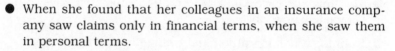

● ● ● Don't judge yourself – judge the situation

Recognising where the situation has been deficient against our needs is an important part of acknowledging our being. It helps us to move away from a sense of career built on 'oughts', against which we may well be deficient, to a career built on internal needs. It also eases the internal dialogue between wants and needs. The 1980s shaped many to believe that wanting a more prestigious company car, a gold charge card, and a biannual mortgage increase were important because they reflected career success; ergo their disappearance in the 1990s implies reduced career success. The finding meaning model allows us to disentangle our wants and needs, to see whether achieving career success can be defined in new ways, which take away guilt and a sense of inadequacy.

Be kinder to yourself

We may have little difficulty in giving our esteem to others, recognising their value and treating them with respect and friendship, but have the utmost difficulty in offering that same esteem to ourselves. Any exercise which asks group members to give a message to another about what they have enjoyed and valued in them during the course of a workshop is entered into with great enthusiasm. Participants want to give others recognition, because they know how good it is to receive positive messages. They also know how difficult it is to recognise aspects of ourselves which may be visible to others. Take away the group prop and ask each individual to say what about themselves they have enjoyed or contributed and the discomfort is palpable. Eyes are downcast, an uneasy silence reigns until social pressures force one person to admit reluctantly that they recognise something of value in themselves. The unspoken rule is that the claim will never be a large one.

The truth is we need both kinds of esteem. We need the recognition of others, but we must start with a recognition of ourselves, since we are the only certain traveller on our career journey.

We need to know what we appreciate in ourselves, unconditionally. Most of us would not swap being ourselves for another person, no matter how visibly successful, which implies that somewhere in our inner core we value ourselves for what we are. As poet Edith Sitwell once said of her striking appearance, 'Why not be yourself? If one is a greyhound why try to look like a pekinese?' Self-appreciation means being willing to accept as central to yourself those attributes which have made you what you are. Ask yourself, these four questions. The only rule in answering them is that they must not refer directly to any qualification or job that you have ever held.

1 What are you good at being?

2 What things are most important to you?

3 Which of your personal skills do you value most (this may not be the same as others would see in you)?

4 What do you like about yourself (even if others don't)?

Answering these questions is a means of adding to the value of your inner cv. Just as building the value of personal market-ability required adding on a quarterly basis to your asset-based cv, so building the strength of your inner core means regularly asking questions of yourself. Answering them may add to your confidence in externally presenting yourself, but more import-antly they help anchor your decisions against your own needs.

Be with others who are like you?

Networking as a career management tool is a well-recognised tactic. 'Old Boys Clubs' are long known as effective means by which older men shape chosen younger colleagues; teach them how to model organisational values and ease career paths. They found their 1980s extensions in the growth of mentoring schemes and the emergence of women's professional networks, as means of women helping each other break through the 'glass ceiling'. In the 1990s the need for networking is being shouted even louder. Tom Peters offers the formula that job security is now proportional to:

1 The thickness of your Rolodex (or filofax or computer database).

2 The rate of its expansion.

3 The share of entries from outside the organisation.

4 The time devoted to its maintenance.

Networking is a key element in keeping you in touch with people who may have power to help you at some future time (and whom you may help in turn). It is essential for those who are looking to build their own business and need constantly to be looking for signs as to where work may be on offer, or where opportunities may be created. It is equally important for organisational careerists as a means not only of finding career supporters, but also for ensuring they know what is happening around them. From an inner core perspective, a network is crucial for sustaining your sense of self. As much as networking is about being with people who model what you aspire to be, or who can give you what you want to have, from an internal perspective it is about being with people who are like you and with whom you can connect.

● ● ● Networking for the inner core

When I asked a now successful entrepreneur why his first attempt had failed, he saw his failure not in terms of lack of business contacts, but in the lack of contact with others like himself. It was difficult to believe he could be what he had the skills to be, because he knew no one living his life. Second time round he consciously sought out others dealing with the same issues, and found comfort and affirmation in their company. For him a network was not primarily an arena for trading business cards, but a place of safety, where he could own up to the pressures and fears he faced. When American careers expert Barbara Sher writes of the importance of a 'network of helping hands behind every genuine success', she is writing as much of the helping hands that affirm the inner self as their ability to help fix things for someone in need.

Networking at its most powerful is genuine concern about the well being of others, and not superficial cocktail party mingling, where everyone looks to attach themselves to someone more powerful. When the European Women's Management Development Network surveyed its members across the globe, they found that for the British the importance of developing genuine social contacts as a prelude to doing business was greater than it was for American members. For the British, a network was a place of safety, in which self-confidence could be built, rather than an arena for self-projection. Culturally, we want rapport before we start trading. Internally, we need a network of rapport as a means of sustaining our sense of self. Being part of a network, to which we feel we belong, provides a sense of balance. It both affirms we are not alone in our needs, and gives us the opportunity to practice being who we want to be. Within your own networks:

● Are they chosen on the basis of being with people whom you enjoy, or with an exclusive eye to the career/business contacts?

● Do you see your network contacts as primarily an insurance policy against unemployment?

● Do you deliberately focus your networking on those who model where you want to be?

● Are you involved in any network either formally or informally which allows you to bring your inner self?

207

You may use different networks for different purposes. Or it may have become apparent that you resist anything approaching a formal network, but have well-developed informal contacts that meet your needs. Alternately, you may have found that your networking is externally focused and avoids ever getting close to your inner core needs.

A skilled networker is one who recognises the need for networks that feed their outer and inner self: that help support their career success and help them find meaning. For some people the networks will be clearly divided, a professional body will serve one need and their church or counselling group another. For some, such as Gillian Edwards, the two are closely entwined.

● ● ● Gillian Edwards: a career built on finding meaning and creating networks

Gillian Edwards is a visible powerhouse of energy and enthusiasm. A friend describes her as a 'one woman community', as she juggles three separate jobs and offers her home as a network base for activities as diverse as art classes and parental guidance. Yet, the story of her attempts at succeeding in a conventional career is one of trying to do the right thing and failing. She dropped out of a languages degree because of a failed relationship, and in the running away became aware of her need to work creatively. She chose to go to Dartington College, a well-known centre for the creative arts, and trained as a drama teacher, only to discover she hated teaching in schools. She resigned and her next years were spent in the quest of 'what am I going to be?'. The journey took her from teaching English as a foreign language to occasional acting jobs, acting as a driver for Pink Floyd, working as PA to a solicitor, and selling high price vacuum cleaners in Scotland. The jobs always seemed to come to her through friends, rather than being sought, while all the time she was searching for how she could find meaning. She spent much time attending workshops and therapy groups, and learnt that the importance of the courses was not that she discovered what she should be doing, but that they led her to people who inspired her – people she wanted to be with.

The nadir of her career fortunes came at a point when her job, home and relationship conspired to disappear at the same time. She was faced with the recognition that she had no idea how to run her life. As often happens at such points she found a book which said something to her. The book *A Course in Miracles*, told her to stop trying to be in control. Instead to try to see what was happening as lessons to learn from, to follow the signs that came to her and to trust that her needs would be taken care of.

Within a month she had a flat, a new relationship and a job, but the story was not neatly tied up. There were plenty more set backs to come. She spent time travelling in Java, found herself dreading the idea of coming back to England, and devised the idea of opening a centre in Southern France – a holiday home where single parents could come with their children for a break, support and learning. She paid a deposit and returned to the UK thinking her future was clear. The possibility of success and meaning seemed to have connected. Six months later when she returned, the dream had turned sour. The house was close to an abattoir and viewed in the cold foggy damp of midwinter its charms were slight. Rather than ignore her intuitions, she acted on them and withdrew from the sale. She was back to square one.

Further attempts at teaching English to foreign students in Oxford proved depressing. A move with a friend to do the same in Florence was no less unhappy. She did, however, recognise her acting skills, in that neither employer suspected that the professional woman who talked her way into both jobs was living in penury in a campervan on the edge of town. When she returned to the UK, she finally accepted that she could not carry on this way and that when she gave up on teaching jobs it wasn't because of lack of skill, it was because the situation wasn't right. She decided that she had to start asking for help, and as soon as she started asking, offers came.

An American educationalist friend asked her to help in the running of a new learning centre. The centre would offer par-ental guidance, and teach children rejected by conventional education. She recognised Gillian's skills in marketing, her personal power as an enthuser, and her abilities as a teacher. Having believed she had abandoned teaching, within a short period of time she was involved and loving it. She had found the place that the teacher in her needed to be. Through contacts with a centre for the self-employed, she was offered two days a week work as an administrator. A personal growth centre then asked her to help in the marketing of their programmes. Working initially as a volunteer her success in doubling registrations led her to ask, and be put on the pay roll. Since that time she has also become involved in running monthly acting workshops and promoting the work of an American therapist whom she admires. Her career now had content, but it wasn't until a friend told her that she now held a 'portfolio' career, that her sense of embarrassment at 'doing a bit of this, and a bit of that' disappeared. Suddenly she was legitimated.

A WEEK IN GILLIAN EDWARDS' WORKING LIFE
Monday

Morning	Teaching motivation and study skills to children aged 6–19 in the new learning centre.
Afternoon	Administration for the school putting together the schedule of talks for the summer term.
Evening	Running two groups in parenting skills.

Tuesday

Morning	Teaching.
Afternoon	Administration.
Evening	Talk to parents and counsellors on establishing good working habits in parents and adolescents.

Wednesday

Morning	Career workshop for 15-year-old girls in a local school.
Afternoon	Working with a client at the self-employed centre on how to market her singing workshops.
Evening	Running two parental guidance groups.

Thursday

Day free	A maintenance day for dealing with personal and domestic needs, and thinking about the book she is planning.

Friday

Morning	Teaching.
Afternoon	Administration for the learning centre.
Evening	Hosts a drop in evening for people who have attended workshops by Chuck Spezzano.

Saturday

Afternoon	Rehearsal with Playback Theatre.

The life Gillian has created for herself is not an affluent one.

There are no obvious material symbols of a successful career. Influenced by her Quaker upbringing she follows the maxim 'let us live simply, so that others may live simply'. Yet listening to her describe her working life, it is transparently successful, because it now matches with a set of beliefs and values which guide her choices:

● She has learnt that she is happy when she is giving service. She sees her purpose as helping people to be true to themselves, lead fulfilling lives and to create harmony in their family lives.

● She is able to interweave important aspects of herself, so that her creativity, patience and compassion as a teacher and counsellor, are balanced with her practicality and enthusiasm as a marketing adviser, and her love of risk taking and showing off as an actor.

● She is able to balance activities which earn her money with giving time to activities which are important to her, but which will not earn money in the immediate future.

● She has learnt that receiving and giving are important parts of achieving goals. That her focus on independence as a sign of maturity stopped her from being able to recognise that being what she needed to be would come through others. That connectedness to others is pivotal to her being able to succeed.

● She is skilful in concentrating on the thing in hand and being in the present – not worrying 'what next?' She now also knows that she is good at what she does.

● She has a strong sense of trust in herself, in other people, and in life itself.

● She chooses to work with people with whom she can identify, so that work seems like fun, and those same people provide springboards for new developments in her career.

Gillian's story is one which could probably only be told so clearly by someone who has spent considerable time thinking about what they need to create in their lives in order to experience success. It may seem a long way away from the structure of your working life. It may even seem like the self-indulgence of a single woman with no responsibilities. I don't believe it is. Through a painful process of years when her career was a 'failure', she has found a set of principles which allow her to remain balanced against the vicissitudes which have always marked unconventional careers. Her willingness to flex, to remain open to letting in new possibilities, to add and remove pieces from her portfolio, and to use her network of like-minded people as the base for building career possibilities, are themes which are as relevant to the organisational careerist as to the self-employed.

Most fundamental of all, however, there is a clear connection in her career success between doing and being. It would be difficult to find where one stops and the other starts. For many conventional careerists the gap has been purposely wide, and the cause of many mid-life reassessments. Contracting and recontracting our career for the future demands that we keep both in sight, as without them we are unbalanced to manage uncertainty.

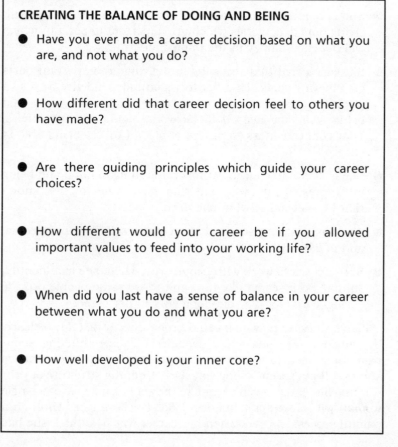

CREATING THE BALANCE OF DOING AND BEING

- Have you ever made a career decision based on what you are, and not what you do?

- How different did that career decision feel to others you have made?

- Are there guiding principles which guide your career choices?

- How different would your career be if you allowed important values to feed into your working life?

- When did you last have a sense of balance in your career between what you do and what you are?

- How well developed is your inner core?

Remember

☐ The 'feel good' factor cannot be sustained through looking to the external environment to make it right for us. When economic cycles are getting shorter, the best source of creating and sustaining a 'feel good' factor is the individual creating their own sense of personal security.

☐ We all need a sense of our own power. That created by position is often transitory, and ill equips people for working in flatter organisations. That created by the person is more sustainable, but needs to extend beyond a reliance on professional expertise. Much personal power lies in the head of the individual. It can be claimed and utilised, or ignored and feed into a sense of powerlessness.

☐ Developing the inner core is as important to sustaining a sense of self as focusing on the externals of knowledge and skills acquisition.

☐ Future career contracts have to be with the self as much as with employers. Ensuring that contract balances the individual's need for career success and their need for meaning are central to careers having a sense of renewal and progression.

☐ Sustaining the inner core is better served by recognising what needs each of us has for being. Traditional career rewards may tell us what we come to want, but not what we need.

☐ We need to ensure our networks place us in touch with those who can support our external and internal career.

☐ A network has too often been seen as a climbing frame, when it can also be our safety net.

" *The easier you make it for others to champion your new deal, the greater are the chances of succeeding.* **"**

13

time to negotiate

'Let us never negotiate out of fear. But let us never fear to negotiate.'
President John F. Kennedy

You can put it off no longer. You've monitored yourself and the world around you. You are now better informed about yourself and the context of your work. You may have come through a discomforting time of uncertainty and now recognise what it is you need. You have the vision, but now it's time for action, and that action requires you to start neg-

"You want a new deal, but you don't want to have to deal."

otiating. At this point your anxiety level starts to rise. You want a new deal, but you don't want to deal. Since without negotiation you will fail to move forward, we need to find a model of negotiation with which you can feel comfortable.

We negotiate every day of our lives. We negotiate over which film to see, what food to eat, who will pick up the children from school, and which parents to visit at Christmas. We recognise that negotiating the price of a house carries more consequences than negotiating for a souvenir in a souk, yet we may dread both. Many negotiations pass unnoticed, but suggest negotiating on a career issue and one model springs to mind. Suddenly, we are in a smoke filled room with management on one side of the table and the trade union on the other. We are in the world of positional bargaining, where wills are in collision, relative powers are constantly being assessed, and the outcome will at best be a compromise.

● ● ● The positional bargain

In a positional negotiation the dialogue has established rules:

Manager I need five extra staff. We are collapsing under the pressure of work. We can't go on like this (which means we need two extra staff, but if I say so I'll get none).

Boss Sorry, you can't have any. You know we are way over budget. You should have put in your claim at the start of the year (which means I know you are overworked and need a couple more staff, but if I admit it you'll think I am a push over).

Manager I have got to have some more staff, or I'll stop all work on processing invoices. Two would be a start. (If I threaten to stop money coming in, that will give me a strong negotiation position).

Boss I know things aren't easy, I shouldn't promise anything this year – but as it's you, I'll find the money for a part timer over the next six months, and then we can look at it again. (If he accepts that one, I've got off well).

Manager Well, if that's the best you can offer now, I'll accept it as a start.

The outcome is classic compromise – both sides can claim a partial victory, but what have they won? The department's work overload will not be solved by a part timer. The underlying problem has not been addressed. The budget will still be overspent. All that has been achieved is that the two parties can comfort themselves that their working relationship is intact. These two parties were anxious to placate, so they backed off from collision and avoided clashing egos. Often neither party in such negotiations will back off, or one side uses the other's desire to avoid conflict as their means of avoiding ceding anything of importance. It's a model that can result in outcomes of little value to either party. It's win-win at a minimal level of gain.

●●● Principled negotiations

An alternative approach to career negotiations is that developed by Roger Fisher and William Ury in the Harvard Negotiation Project. They identified that negotiations always take place at two levels:

- **Substance** – what is being negotiated for.
- **Process** – how the negotiation is conducted.

Principled negotiation looks at issues on their merits, recognises the position of both parties and looks to find outcomes which are simultaneously wise, efficient and maintaining of relationships. It is in close accord with the principles for career dealing because it is concerned with:

- separating people out from the problem being discussed.
- establishing the underlying interests of both parties.
- generating options rather than having fixed positions.
- identifying objective criteria for assessing options.

To these four principles add two others:

- A focus on the future.
- The monitoring of outcomes.

●●● The people factor

You have probably played the internal dialogue game, where you practice in your head the conversation which will follow your request for a pay rise, job change, promotion, etc. Invariably the actual conversation has little point of recognition with your own internal theatre, because yours was based on your own model of thinking. If you like being persuaded by appeals to higher concerns, you will have fed that into the dialogue and ready capitulation followed. If it's facts that persuade you, then it's facts you will have given out. We start from our own model, even though the other party's is very different. A common vision interests them little, but understanding the positive and negative consequences for them of agreement, interests them greatly. To negotiate effectively, you have to sit in the other's seat, seeing and feeling the issue from their perspective.

Career negotiator's perspective	Organisational negotiator's perspective
● I am being asked to work too hard.	● I am being asked to work too hard, and any less for him, means more for me.
● My life would be easier if I could work part-time.	● If we are to meet our departmental targets I need everybody I can get my hands on, working at full stretch.
● I have no time for life outside work.	● What life outside work?
● If I worked part-time I would have more time to study, so I can make a career change.	● What sort of effort am I going to get out of a part-time worker who is planning on a career change?

Pursuing a line of negotiation based on individual self-interest is doomed to failure. It's not that this organisational negotiator is unreasonable. They have major concerns of their own, so that any shift from deadlock has to focus on finding arguments that offer the other a benefit. A line of argument developed from sitting in the other's seat could focus on:

● Willingness to negotiate an annual hours contract, so that time input is shaped by the needs of the department.

● Reduced overhead costs that could be used to bring in another part-timer, or to reward full-time colleagues.

● Recognising that your request is part of a broader issue as to how work can be made more manageable for everyone.

Sitting in the other seat is not just an intellectual exercise. It also means recognising the emotions of the other side. They may be equally unhappy with what's happening to their career, angry at those further up the line who are now denying them career options, and envious that you have a possible way out. You may be feeling a power differential because they are your manager. They may be feeling a power differential because you have choices and they don't see any. One way of reducing that differential is to talk with them as an adult, not as an angry child pleading for your own way. See them as a joint problem solver, and bring into the open the concerns which your request raises. Rather than shouting 'Unfair', acknowledge, 'My suggestion potentially creates difficulties for you, at a time when we are fully committed. Can we look at how it would impact on everyone else, and whether there are other possibilities?'

Sit alongside

Metaphorically sitting alongside is more likely to lead to a positive resolution than simply looking to persuade by force of argument. Sitting alongside means identifying benefits to them in acceptance, and accepting the concerns which have to be managed. It also means bringing your career issue as a problem you need help with, rather than presenting a solution to a problem they may not have yet recognised. Start with the answer, 'I have decided that the best option for me is to get a secondment into another division', and before the words are out, they have moved into an internal world where listening has stopped and critical evaluation started. Start with the issue, 'Now that we are working more closely with customers, the narrowness of my experience sometimes makes me ill-equipped for situations I am having to handle', and there is an agenda that asks to be addressed.

● ● ● The underlying interests

In positional bargaining both sides are intent on shouting their position louder than the other (you only have to look at TV coverage during major industrial disputes to see the evidence), but in principled negotiations the focus is on understanding the underlying interests of the other side. An individual asserts their right to promotion, the boss counters with the claim that they should be grateful to have a job. An ill-natured discussion follows and the thwarted employee returns to his desk and calls a recruitment consultancy. However, if they had taken time to discover each other's interests, they could have discovered a way through. The individual wants to be seen as a person who is moving forward in their career, the manager can't afford to be seen as offering promotions at the same time as handing out redundancies.

- The individual may be willing to increase the scope of their job, but without public signalling of the change.

- They may accept being rewarded when they have evidenced the new skills required, rather than being rewarded at the point of entry.

- They may accept being moved into another business area where the climate is more conducive to offering promotions.

- They may be willing to work on a high visibility project as part of their present role, knowing it will bring them into contact with influential senior managers.

Each of these options could also meet the interest of the organisational representative, in that they would not be open to charges of insensitivity. Discovering the interests of the other party can come through inference. Closely listening to what they say and then asking questions of yourself, can disclose the interests they are looking to protect. If they are stonewalling any discussion of promotion, ask yourself, 'How would my being promoted impact on their interests as an individual or as a manager?', or 'Would meeting my request clash with their personal values?' Your answers can give clues as to where their interests lie. It may be possible to bring your questioning into the open through verbalising what you believe they are thinking. 'I sense that you have concerns about the presentational aspects of promoting a staff member at a time like this, am I right?', offers an opportunity to open up. If your assessment is wrong, it's likely you'll then discover what is behind the non-verbal signals of protest they have been sending out.

You don't have to share interests

Understanding others' interests is different from sharing them. Empathy is being called for not sympathy. Shift too far into the other's world and it may be difficult to hold on to a strong belief in your own interests. Fisher and

"Acknowledge the other's world, but don't move into it."

Ury advise that a 'useful rule of thumb is to give positive support to the human beings on the other side, equal in strength to the vigour with which you emphasise the problem'. Acknowledge the other's world, but don't move into it.

There may even be times when recognising that your interests are different can be a help in reaching a goal. When the government established the Child Support Agency their interest was in reducing the cost of state support to single parents. They found a strong ally in groups representing single mothers whose interest was in forcing absent fathers to accept personal responsibility for their children. Their interests were different, but galvanising their combined power enabled a piece of problematic legislation to reach the statute book. Similarly, if you are well informed on the context in which your business is operating, you will be able to identify its interests, ally yours to theirs and increase your negotiating hand as a consequence.

●●● Be creative

Positional bargaining usually centres around two opposing positions and looks to close the gap between them. The principled negotiation process doesn't start from a fixed offering, but instead looks to be creative. There may be several ways in which interests can be met, provided that you have thought before negotiations start, not just about the ways in which your needs could be satisfied, but also as to how their needs could be met through dealing with you. Since it is far easier to think creatively about oneself than the opposing party, it's worthwhile calling on friends to brainstorm on the organisation's behalf. If negotiations falter when the other party believes that what you are wanting is not realisable, but can't put forward any alter-natives, you need to have some thoughts ready as to what else could be offered. It keeps the negotiation moving, and stops the other party from losing face.

●●● Be objective

The reaction to any request for change is often more emotional than rational. Suggest to senior managers that their job could be shared as easily as a secretarial post, and they splutter in indignation. They see the suggestion as a slight on their status, abilities and commitment. They may also recognise that if it was shared, competition from women would increase dramatically. Tell them that a shared post would give a wider range of skills, experiences and thought processes to call on in handling strategic issues; that it would ensure the role was filled all year long; that more business might be won if they could use their differences to work more effectively with the differing styles of clients, and they start to recognise that there could be some pluses. The recognition comes when they are pulled from their emotional and often prejudicial response base into the world of the rational. Given the evidence from the Myers-Briggs Test Inventory that British managers overwhelmingly prefer to deal with facts rather than feelings (even though their decisions are often driven by feelings rather than facts), it is imperative that in career negotiations you establish objective criteria against which options can be assessed. You should establish with your negotiation partner, in advance of disclosure of your preferences, the criteria which will allow for judging options. For example:

● That an option will not cause extra workload for colleagues.

● That the career deal supports the department and organisation in delivering on its objectives.

● That it will not damage service delivery – and could improve it.

● That the new deal will be capable of measurement against performance criteria.

● That before rejecting an option it must be clearly demonstrated that it does not meet an organisational expectation.

● ● ● Monitor

An extension of objectivity is to encourage the organisation to monitor the consequences of a negotiation. You will be assessing whether the outcome is working for you, so suggest that they do the same. If you have argued that the change will not impact on service delivery, then suggest a review after six months. If you have argued that supporting you in studying for an MBA will enable you to make financially better informed decisions, then suggest it is explicitly looked at in your next appraisal. Monitoring will support the development of a climate in which norms can be challenged, provided that they support the organisation's purpose, and also establishes a process for further dealing. The man who negotiates for a period of part-time working may want to renegotiate re-entry to full-time working at a future date. The woman who asks for project work in order to develop teamleading skills may want to strengthen her specialist skills two years on. Establishing a monitoring process helps build the rationale for subsequent negotiations, and encourages acceptance of new options, provided that they can be shown to work.

●●● Focus on the future

It's tempting to use the past as a point of reference, since the past is often full of precedents to support your claims. It's tempting but dangerous. As much as individuals may resent the removal of career offers, the organisation can be equally mourning the loss of a protected market, a strong pound and undemanding shareholders. The past, as L.P. Hartley said, 'is a foreign country, they do things differently there'. Your negotiations have to look at your future and how it can support your employer in its future.

●●● Make it easy for them

Despite this presentation of negotiation as an exchange between two parties, the reality is that a career negotiation will usually require several iterations, as the case is sold up the line or into Personnel. It is important that having used all your skills in winning over your first ally, you do not abandon them to fight your case alone. It may have been your visible commitment which finally persuaded them, but they won't be able to carry the strength of your emotions in selling the case to their boss. If you first sold your case to Personnel, they now have to sell it to your line manager. You now need to think of the interests of the other stakeholders in the decision. Recognising the positions from which your case could be criticised by others can help you in supporting your first 'champion'. Encourage your 'champion' to tell you what help they need in taking the case forward. Is yours an organisation which constantly looks to benchmark, so that they will be asked for evidence of whether competitors are allowing similar deals? If it is then you can start enquiring. Is it one where the bottom line is everything, so that as long as your option cuts costs it is likely to be agreed to? Is it one where precedent is all

223

important, so that discovering that it has already been tried out elsewhere in the organisation (no matter how geographically distant) will instil confidence? The easier you make it for others to champion your new deal, the greater are the chances of its succeeding.

● ● ● Removing the power differentials

'All that's fine, but at the end of the day they have more power than I have', is a common response to the idea of career negotiations. They have position power, they have the power of authority, but you also have sources of power. As a knowledge worker you have the power of expertise, and they risk losing that expertise if they fail to deal. You may have personal power in that you are able to achieve ends because of your ability to attract people to you. Flattening hierarchies means more scope for person power. You may have the power of persuasion and find that people defer to you, even though your official power is slight. Recognise your own power bases, as this will decide where you start your negotiation. Recognise also the power base of those you are dealing with. There is little point focusing your energies on Personnel, if their power to influence is slight. There may, however, be every point in sounding out your ideas with a colleague who is known to have influence over a key decision-maker.

Even if you have difficulty accepting that you have power sources, there are actions you can take which will increase your power.

- **Be prepared to walk away.** Walking away from a market vendor is an established technique for encouraging them to rethink their final price, so be prepared to walk away from negotiations if the situation is in danger of becoming a positional lock-in.

- **Choose your time.** An offer that is rejected one year may be looked at very differently the next, when business circumstances have changed. You may decide to place your career negotiation in the medium rather than the short term, and identify some steps towards that goal. Alternately, you may look to revive a negotiation where previously your thinking was ahead of your employer.

● **Have a back-up plan** so that if you can't get the deal you want you have alternatives. Knowing that your future does not depend on getting this exact deal can give you the inner confidence that increases the likelihood of success. A friend had spent several months negotiating an internal job move to Geneva. As time went on it became clear that the blockage was the financial package which she required in order to make the move feasible. HR's tactic was to let the negotiations slow down in the belief that eventually her desire for the job would drive her to accept their offer. Instead she used the time to investigate alternatives. She explored the job market to see what else was available. She talked with the Head of UK Operations to see whether the job could be UK based with occasional trips to Geneva. She talked with her boss about whether aspects of the Geneva job which appealed to her could be built into her present job, to mutual benefit. Her development of alternatives gave her a sense of power which was lacking when she saw herself as tied to only one option. In the end she rejected the Geneva offer, but she did renegotiate a new role for herself which met her career objectives.

Since your career is going to be a series of negotiations of the psychological contract between you and your employer(s), it's vital that you develop your negotiation skills. Having learnt the rules of principled negotiations which respect your needs and those of your negotiating partners, complete the negotiation grid to see how you need to prepare for your next career negotiation. Until you can complete it, you are not ready to enter the arena.

CAREER NEGOTIATION GRID

What is the career problem I am wanting to resolve?	What options can I see for myself?	What is the organisational benefit of creating a new deal with me?	Who has to be won over, and what are their preferred styles of being influenced?	What will stop them listening to me?	What are their most likely concerns and how will I answer them?	What back-up alternatives do I have in case negotiations do not go as planned?	What objective criteria should be used in considering options?	What is my power base, and how can I maximise it's effectiveness?

Remember

☐ Negotiation is central to career dealing, but it's also the aspect many people feel most discomfort with. Building comfort comes from letting go of a view of negotiation as the locking of wills, where the one with most power wins out. Your negotiations are about moving your career forward through working with the organisational context. It's better achieved sitting alongside than across a table.

☐ The career dealing model is one where both parties look to operate from the principles of recognising the other person's world, focusing on the identification of interests, being willing to explore options rather than defending positions, and using objective criteria for evaluating options.

☐ As an individual you cannot control the organisation's response, but since you are part of the organisational system, a change in how you approach career negotiations will have an effect on the response you get from those you deal with. You can be both a catalyst of change and an agent in the response of others.

☐ Formal power differentials can never be removed, but they can be diminished by focusing on building your power base. Measure the climate, so that you can judge when and when not to open negotiations. Always have back-up alternatives. Knowing they are there will help build an inner strength which will feed into your negotiations.

☐ Having negotiated once you will have learnt a powerful model for managing all future career dealings.

"Employment never pays us enough, but it is 100 per cent more than we are guaranteed when self-employed.**"**

financial dealings

'Don't change the price – change the package.'
Gavin Kennedy

To think about the career deal we want without also considering the financial implications of that choice is impossible. The sense of being financially tied into an organisation contributes to the sense of entrapment which I often hear in employees. Ironically, the very incentives which their organisations put in place in order to motivate continued commitment (when relational dealing was the order of the day) are now helping to retain reluctant individuals under the transactional deal. Where else are they going to get such a generous mortgage subsidy, where else will their pension be based on such a high percentage of final salary? It's because financial rewards are no longer matching organisational needs that they have to change. In the posttransactional world, new financial deals will emerge which must also meet the more individualised needs of individuals.

In the past the financial dealing rules were clear. The further up the pyramid one climbed, the greater were the rewards. It was a perfect motivational system for those who followed linear careers. It was job size which decided salary, car size, length of holiday and even where you ate. In its more recent reinterpretations, individual performance has become an element in the package, with more senior managers being placed on individual contracts which offer bonus payments and share options, while more junior staff accept performance related-pay as the basis of reward.

Organisations are now realising that the shift from pay for length of time in job to reward for performance isn't working. Introduced as a signal that the deal was now contingent on work output not time input, it has faltered as a motivator because it only goes part of the way. In a low inflation economy, and at a time of business squeeze, asking a manager to motivate his team by dividing up a 3 per cent salary pool is a time-consuming exercise with little pay off. Paradoxically, the manager needs to retain some visible underperformers in order to be able to make any meaningful distinctions between staff. A 3 per cent increase employee is unlikely to come through the door each day with more enthusiasm than the 2 per cent colleague. While 67 per cent of UK companies now use performance-related pay schemes, their inadequacies are beginning to be acknowledged. Those who have to administer them complain that they take up large amounts of time and, in reality, are primarily being used as means of controlling the salary bill. Those who are in receipt of them complain that the rewards are insufficient to make a difference. While job motivation comes from more than pay, if pay is used as a means of motivation it has to work.

● ● ● New financial deals

For financial dealing to be part of the invisible handshake, it has to be rethought. We know that the need of the organisation is for visible contribution, continuous learning, and commitment to task and team. It makes no sense to continue to offer rewards which focus on the job title and reward most those who have been there longest. It makes no sense for rewards to be hierarchically based if the hierarchy is increasingly flat. This simply continues to encourage linear career expectations, when many able employees will have organisational careers of limited vertical progression. They will be developing, moving across areas, acquiring in-depth knowledge, and accepting new responsibilities. How is this to be reflected in their rewards? Increasing the pool for performance-related pay is unlikely to be sufficient. Most PRP schemes make an overall assessment of performance against broad criteria. Have the objectives set at last year's appraisal been met? Has the individual met the role requirements of their job? The system assumes that individuals operate in isolation to each other. If I fail to meet an objective it's my fault alone, and if I succeeded I did it all by myself.

Since team working and projects are the new mantra, reward systems will have to reflect that shift. If the employer doesn't want people to see themselves as job holders hanging on to a job description, they will have to reward them against the competences they are displaying. More of the reward will need to be based on the output of the team and the business unit. Why shouldn't a team be rewarded when it completes an assignment ahead of time? Why shouldn't their reward be linked to the profitability of their particular business unit, and not to the overall performance of a large organisation, from whom they may feel very distant? From the organisation's side it makes little sense to try and motivate performance through offering rewards based on the overall performance of the company if large parts of it are consistently underperforming. Plc performance may motivate those on track for the board, but it has little meaning for those with different ambitions.

Valuing intellectual assets

What may make better sense is to offer share options to knowledge workers in order to encourage them to 'buy in' to the company. International management consultancy PA now requires of senior staff that part of their bonus is taken in shares. Chief Executive Jon Moynihan's rationale is that since the only assets a consultancy has are intellectual, it makes business sense to encourage the retention of the most valuable. This approach is reinforced by the evidence that the market value of the top 200 businesses on the London Stock Exchange is on average three times greater than the worth of their visible fixed assets. The invisible assets are the 'know how' of the people who contribute to the success of those enterprises.

The financial logic of what organisations are now asking of their employees is that financial dealing should become increasingly differentiated. Pay will become disconnected from the job and more strongly connected to the contribution of the person. Once that break is made then a new dialogue opens up.

The individual deal

The deals which organisations have traditionally offered have been modelled on meeting the needs of a nuclear family unit. They have rewarded continuous service. They have rewarded establishing a home. They have assumed marriage and that establishing long-term financial security is a high priority. They have assumed that earning needs are highest in the 30s and 40s when children are still dependent, and that vacations are most valued by those with most service. All of these assumptions can be challenged. Many families are now headed by women who have not had continuous service. Many younger people do not want to commit to home ownership. Heterosexual couples choose not to marry, and gay employees have partners. A young single person may be more cash hungry than a middle aged one whose parents' death has allowed them to discharge their mortgage. Longer holidays may be valued by those with least service, and childcare help may be of more benefit than a company car.

For benefits to earn an organisational return, they have to be valued by those to whom they are offered. A local employer continues to offer service rewards, in gifts of increasing value, all of which are emboldened with the company's logo. The gifts are still valued by older employees who see them as vestiges of the relational deal. Younger employees howl with derision when the gift catalogue is circulated around the office. In the post-transactional world, benefits have to be matched against the individual needs of employees, or they will fail to motivate the performance that is expected in return.

Flexible benefits

The recognition that flexibility is a two-way stretch is coming. Benefits consultancy Gissings reported in 1995 that only 8 per cent of companies operate flexible benefits schemes, but nine out of ten firms surveyed by management consultancy William M Mercer state that they intend to do so. Within five to ten years, job evaluation experts Hay MSL believe, flexible benefits will be commonplace. What has slowed down their introduction has been the difficulty of HR administrating individualised packages, but spreadsheet software is now removing those problems. The mental and practical blockages to the idea of allowing individuals to 'pick and mix' benefits to an agreed value are starting to crumble.

Mercury Communications as a recent entrant to the telecommunications sector has 10,000 employees with an average age of 31. They have accepted flexible packages in recognition that a 31 year old can be a married man with two children, a single parent, a double income partnership or a firmly unattached individual. Each employee values different benefits. A single person in their twenties wants cash, and time to travel. In their thirties they may prefer to trade long-term protection for a car allowance. In their forties they may be looking for healthcare cover and larger payments into their pension plan.

When Walker Snack Foods surveyed employees on what they would want available in a tailored package, benefits expanded to include dental care, disability protection, childcare payments and life assurance. When the scheme was introduced, over half the employees opted to change their package. While pension, company car, life and medical assurance will probably continue to be the most valued benefits, a clue to the future can be seen in the USA where home security systems are now included in options menus.

No longer on offer

Alongside offerings are withdrawals. When American Express ended their mortgage subsidy scheme, they were heralding both that long-term financial tie-ins are no longer desirable from the company's perspective, and acknowledging that for many younger employees acquiring an mortgage is ceasing to be a career motivator. Apple Computing in choosing not to operate a pension scheme, is signalling that it wants employees to join them when they are unconcerned about pensions and to leave when they assume a high priority. The 'package' has been a much envied feature of large organisations. As organisations are recognising their disbenefits, we can expect that offers will be targeted at those on whom the organisation has greatest dependence for performance. Since small organisations will be the areas of greatest growth in employment and have never taken the same role of financial protector, individuals will be increasingly responsible for their own financial management. According to Fiona Price, a leading independent financial adviser, 'People have to learn to adapt. They need to change their mind set. If people don't face facts, then they don't create their own financial independence, and they will become severely disadvantaged.'

> **Ask yourself**
>
> ● Are you currently paid for the skills you bring to your work, or for the job that you hold?
>
> ● What in your benefits package do you place most and least value on?
>
> ● What would you be willing to trade?
>
> ● Are there offerings which you don't presently receive which would act as a motivator to high performance?
>
> ● Do you know the value of the package which you currently hold – and therefore how much you would need to be offered if you moved to a 'cash only' employer?

Knowing the answers to these questions will help you in negotiations on your next career deal. The world of individualised dealing is one with which trade unions have yet to come to terms with. They are still focusing on a world of collectivism inside organisations, when the world inside is shrinking and increasingly non-collective, and the world outside is fragmented but growing. The unwillingness or inability of trade unions to work with new organisational structures is one of the reasons why individuals have to take more responsibility for monitoring their own financial deal.

● ● ● The deal on the outside

The benefits package for those outside the organisation is both simpler and more complex – simpler in that every element of the package will be decided by the individual according to their own preferences and resources, and more complex in that the life choice is part of the benefits package. A former colleague, now well established in his own company, advises others considering the change to start by identifying the car they want to be seen driving. In his personal package, visible status markers have a high place. Another colleague places a high value on being able to live in Spain for parts of each year. A third drives herself hard, and then rewards herself with regular trips to a health farm and time off with friends. Their benefit packages are as individualised as they are, but underpinning them is the need to provide a level of income that makes choice possible. Even more than the organisational worker their pay is performance related. Their benefits are on offer to the degree that they can sell their skills.

● ● ● Assessing the deal

In working with those who are considering self-employment and are concerned about how they can continue to provide the benefits of company life that they have become accustomed to, Fiona Price asks clients to assess the rate they need to charge for their work. The charging rate calculation is based on the formula:

CHARGING RATE CALCULATION

Annual living expenses	£ . . . .
Business expenses (exclusive of capital equipment costs)	£ . . . .
Costs of running car	£ . . . .
Pension contributions	£ . . . .
Payments for replaced benefits	£ . . . .
Holiday costs	£ . . . .
Provision for tax bill	£ . . . .
Total income required	£ . . . .
Total numbers of days available	£ . . . .
Daily rate (1/2)	£ . . . .

Completing the charging rate calculation can be a salutary experience. It makes apparent just how much we have come to expect while an employee. Once a realistic assessment of how many fee earning days are available in a year (when allowance is made for selling time, administration, marketing, client relationship building, self-development and networking, not forgetting holidays and illness), then the high value of what a peripheral employee has to offer clients, in order to achieve the financial deal they seek, is spotlighted. The relationship between input and output is stark.

The calculation gives an overall figure, but what if, like Phil Bunnell, you want to work with clients who can pay little or nothing, because you can see other benefits in association? That choice has immediate consequences for your daily rate and for defining the clients who will see your figure as within their price range. Calculate the rate you would need to charge and then ask yourself how confident you are that it compares well with those with whom you would be competing for work?

● ● ● The foundations of a self-employed package

A straight transfer of the corporate package to self-employment is not realisable for most in the first few years. That is why the invisible benefits have to be put in the scales and weighed along-side. As a financial adviser, Fiona Price works with the self-employed in helping them identify where their priorities lie. Her advice is that for a self-employed deal to be satisfactory, it has to focus simultaneously on short- and long-term needs, leaving the medium-term benefits for the better times. The need is to assess how much an individual can afford to spend on building protection – using that figure to establish how much needs to be immediately available for emergencies, and how much can be put towards the long-term protection of pensions, life assurance policies and illness protection policies. Any extra money can then be used for other savings plans and perks that were once taken for granted. It is notable how often the person who spent hours quibbling with Personnel over their right to a new car will happily accept driving an aging mass market model, once they are no longer career competing in the car park. Their benefits package has shifted its dimensions.

The Autonomy Audit (see Chapter 9) may have highlighted that the risk of financial insecurity is the key disincentive towards change. The ability to input into policies and pensions in lump sums, when earnings are higher, rather than being tied to regular payments is one means of controlling the sense of insecurity. However, until mortgage providers flex their policies so that payment patterns can reflect the changing rhythms of working lives, home ownership will continue to stand as a barrier to many being able to contemplate the switch. For those considering working outside an organisation, it is important to be clear on the financial deal that is being sought.

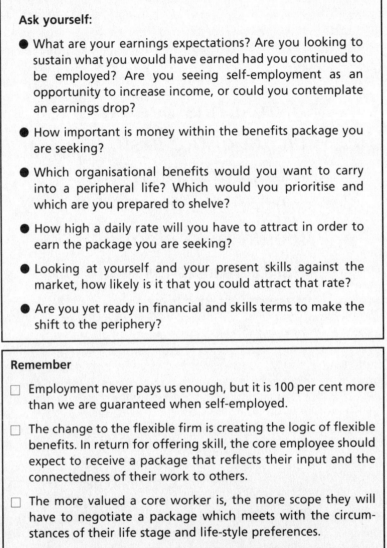

Ask yourself:

● What are your earnings expectations? Are you looking to sustain what you would have earned had you continued to be employed? Are you seeing self-employment as an opportunity to increase income, or could you contemplate an earnings drop?

● How important is money within the benefits package you are seeking?

● Which organisational benefits would you want to carry into a peripheral life? Which would you prioritise and which are you prepared to shelve?

● How high a daily rate will you have to attract in order to earn the package you are seeking?

● Looking at yourself and your present skills against the market, how likely is it that you could attract that rate?

● Are you yet ready in financial and skills terms to make the shift to the periphery?

Remember

☐ Employment never pays us enough, but it is 100 per cent more than we are guaranteed when self-employed.

☐ The change to the flexible firm is creating the logic of flexible benefits. In return for offering skill, the core employee should expect to receive a package that reflects their input and the connectedness of their work to others.

☐ The more valued a core worker is, the more scope they will have to negotiate a package which meets with the circumstances of their life stage and life-style preferences.

☐ Those who work on the periphery have to create their own benefits package. It will have both tangible and intangible elements, with earnings being either a high benefit, or a trade off against other gains.

☐ Whether employed or self-employed, the financial dealing message is one of growing independence.

"*If trust has been a victim of the last few years, then career dealing would be a clear action towards recreating that trust.***"**

start career dealing

*'Trust is a delicate property of human relationships.
It is influenced far more by actions than by words.
It takes a long time to build but it can be destroyed
very quickly.'*
Douglas McGregor

In the months since I started writing, the climate within the UK
has changed. Shareholders are campaigning against the pay of
their chief executive; economists
are talking of the need for a moral
economy where the human consequences of policy making are
considered alongside the financial; and a new term has entered
the management phrasebook
'loyalty management'. Every-
where there are signals that the one-sidedness of the relationship between employer and employee is beginning to be
challenged.

> **"a new term has
> entered the
> management
> phrasebook 'loyalty
> management'."**

●●● A new business secret – loyalty!

There is a moral outrage that those at the top of organisations
can separate out their fate from those who create its wealth.
There is concern that in creating a lean and mean workplace we
create a society which is mean to those without work, who will
in turn be mean to those who have it. We are seeing
organisations begin to put a price on the loss of loyalty. In a
Radio 4 news report, David Owen, Group HR Director of Forte,
announced that when an organisation has a satisfied loyal
workforce, customers sense it and respond by coming back
again and again. When the potential value of a regular customer

at a Little Chef outlet is £10–£15,000 over a lifetime, it starts to make hard bottom-line sense to encourage employee loyalty. That staff loyalty creates customer loyalty should hardly be news. We like to see the same faces when we come back to do business. Confidence is inspired and a sense that it is not just a business exchange, but a relationship which we have with the shopkeeper, financial adviser or doctor. Encouraging loyalty goes even further than keeping staff in order to keep customers happy. As 3M have discovered, loyalty encourages a climate in which employees feel safe to innovate and take risks. HR Development Manager, Paul Davies, claims that, 'People are more likely to feel good about taking risks if they feel secure.' Andersen Consulting, in looking at 71 automotive plants world-wide, found that world-class performance in terms of efficiency and quality was found in those plants with the most experienced employees. Even BT, now an annual presence in the announcement of redundancies, is moving away from the large-scale use of contract workers and back to offering permanent contracts. The message is starting to get through that unilaterally changing the deal can have business consequences that undermine the very reasons for making the change. The challenge for organisations is how to recreate a sense of loyalty without going back to the limitations of the old deal.

● ● ● Have the figures been wrong?

There are those who are questioning the future workplace as one of flexible workers and growing impermanence. They argue that lifelong employment was only ever the privilege of a few specialist industries, such as mining and printing; that part-time work grew faster in the 1960s than it has in the 1990s, and that only 6.5 per cent of employees are on temporary contracts. If 37 per cent of men had been with their employers for 10 years or more in 1968, the figure had only dropped to 36 per cent by 1993. In other words, the pervading sense of insecurity is a misplaced part of an end of millennium mood of crisis. Don't believe the employment 'Cassandras' of the media, they urge; it never really was that different from how it is now. In one sense they may be right. Employment predictions are notoriously inaccurate, but there is other evidence which argues against complacency. If employees were more promiscuous in moving from job to job in the 1960s and 1970s, they could do so because of a Welfare

State which they knew would support them during times of unemployment. That Welfare State has been radically altered, largely because of growing unemployment, so that access to it is both more difficult and less generous. Seven out of ten managers have gone through organisational restructuring in the past two years according to a 1994 Institute of Management Survey, and between 25 per cent and 33 per cent of the workforce have gone through a period of unemployment in the past few years.

Statistically, if you haven't directly experienced unemployment, it's likely to have touched your life in some way. Even if managers have had the same ten years of employment as their predecessors, their mood at the end of those ten years is far different. The manager of the 1960s could have confidence in a continued career, the manager of the 1990s may be staying because of no confidence that they could find work elsewhere. Figures only tell half the story. The real message of the 1990s has been one of worker anxiety.

Put the two messages together: a growing desire by organisations to recreate a sense of loyalty, and a growing sense of insecurity among those who remain, and there is a yawning gap. Bridging it means recreating a sense of mutual trust.

● ● ● Recreating trust

This loss of trust in the organisation has been an unspoken by-product of the last few years. Trust is something that isn't spoken of when it's present, because it can be assumed. Trust is invisible but is made visible in actions. It's the knowledge based on precedent that people get taken care of when they are in trouble, that a manager will always defend his workers, that promises once made will be kept. Trust is based on the consistency of keeping commitments and promises. When actions are taken which contradict those beliefs, then trust goes. For employers, employees' loss of trust is being made visible in low staff morale. Greater attention is now being given to staff attitude surveys. Where negative findings were once quickly explained away and then lost in filing cabinets, they are now being seen as important business indicators. Organisations are setting objectives for improving staff morale as part of their annual business plan, and they know that the answers do not lie in the traditional welfare gestures of social events, good service awards and a company newsletter. Trust has to be rebuilt.

Trust can be regained. If it was built over time in response to one set of conditions, there is no reason why it cannot be rebuilt for another. Adherence to the principles, not the context, is important. The principles of trust are ongoing. For trust to be given, the giver has to perceive the other as:

● worthy of their reliance
● truthful
● having integrity
● accepting of responsibility
● competent
● inspiring of confidence

No employee is going to give their trust to an organisation which it can see is incompetent in running its business, no matter how charismatic its leader. They will simply see assertions of confidence as untruthful and lacking in integrity. An employee can, however, give their trust to an organisation which follows the principles of career dealing:

● **Information** about the present and future business of the organisation is shared.
● **Information** about an employee's performance and the reality of their future is given.
  Consequence
● Employees can believe in the organisation as **truthful**. They may not like what they hear, but they are clear that there is not a parallel world of truth to which they are denied access. Having access to truth puts choices about the future back in individuals' hands.

● **Negotiate** – The organisation is willing to negotiate about career options.
● The organisation sees employee and employer as equal **negotiation partners**.
  Consequence
  Employees see the organisation as acting with **integrity**. It is both modelling that the organisation is no longer the owner of the individual's career, and it is accepting that self-management should not be unsupported.

● **Monitoring** the outcome of career deals is built into the process, so that they are regularly reviewed to ensure they still meet business need.

- The organisation ensures that individuals are given opportunities to **monitor** themselves against the changing environment.

Consequence

The individual sees the organisation as **competent**, because agreements are based on business need, and are monitored against that need, rather than being based on individual prejudice, favoured status, or lack of precedent.

- **Renegotiation** occurs throughout a career because of change in either the organisation or the individual.
- The organisation is willing to renegotiate for **changing positions** within the core and the periphery, and does not see exit as precluding re-entry at a later time.

Consequence

The individual comes to believe that the organisation is **reliable** rather than vengeful, and that they can have **confidence** in an ongoing and changing relationship with it. They come to see that changes in the workplace can be allied to changes in themselves to mutual benefit. If trust has been a victim of the last few years, then career dealing would be a clear action towards recreating that trust.

● ● ● Trust yourself

The time is right for organisations to pay attention to rebuilding trust, without denying the degree of change that they have continuously to live with. Their willingness to career deal can only be a true partnership if you are able to trust yourself as an equal. As much as I have argued the need to recognise what is now being required of you, I have also urged you to trust in yourself. You are the most reliable guide to the deal you need to create for yourself (no matter how different it may look from the career you have followed so far, or from the careers of those around you). To create that deal requires you to build the sense of trust in yourself, which was visible in all those who told me their career stories. Each one of them is succeeding in the career deal they have created because as much as they have learnt how to deal with the world of external opportunities, they have learnt to work with their inner self:

Self-knowledge

They have come to accept and work with the guiding values and principles which shape their lives – rather than fighting against them in order to have a 'proper career'. They are clear about their strengths, but not blind to their weaknesses. They use those insights to shape the life they lead, rather than to punish themselves for what they are not.

Direction

They don't have a lifelong goal. They are not politicians asserting Downing Street as their target while still students. Instead, they have an overall sense of personal direction, which they constantly revisit. Just as an automatic pilot is only accurately on course for 2 per cent of its journey and needs constant adjustments from its human pilot, so these individuals take time to monitor themselves against where they see themselves heading. In the monitoring they may find a new route that is more interesting, or see that the route ahead is blocked but that there are other ways around. Stating an unswerving career goal can be less a sign of determination than of self-defeatism. Far better to know your general direction, but be open to discovering new paths.

Positive approach

All of my interviewees had a positive approach to life. Regardless of the vicissitudes which they had faced, they still saw life and their work as exciting. They had an expectation that it should bring them enjoyment and should add to their whole self, rather than being a drain on their real being. They were willing to trust others because they had a sense of trust in themselves. They believed that, regardless of the unpredictabilities of the economy, they would find a way of working with it, because of their skills and personal competence.

Self-esteem

In talking with each of them it was obvious that they valued themselves. They were not boastful or arrogant. They were not large egos shouting for attention, they were healthy egos, centred within themselves. They each gave a sense of believing in the worth of what they did, and were unlikely to be knocked by the suspicion or cynicism of others. They were anchored by a belief in their own value, which gave them strength in dealing with uncertainties.

Written like this it sounds as though I am writing about superpeople, products of perfect parenting or years of therapy. I am not. I am describing people who were very different in many aspects of their lives and personalities, but who were united in having learnt to trust themselves as the basis for career dealing. They were no different in their capabilities than many of the unhappy individuals I have encountered in my research work. They were different in having a sense of personal control. I don't believe they are more capable than you are, they just started to deal earlier.

● ● ● Listen to that inner voice

You will know when it is the time for you to start moving towards your new career deal, you will have within you messages that demand positive action:

Not I can't bear it any more around here, it's so badly managed.
But I can do better than this, and I can show them how.

Not They would never allow me to do that.
But I can show them why it makes sense for me to do that.

Not I could do it, but they've never let a woman work overseas before.
But I can be the first woman to work overseas.

Not Working part time is career death, so there's no point considering it.
But Why should I be marginalised if I work part time, provided that I ensure my part-time work is meaningful, and that I can renegotiate re-entry to full time.

Not If they say 'No' to me, that's it, I'm trapped here.
But If they say 'No' to me, then I'll take my request elsewhere. They would be stupid to waste my experience.

When your inner dialogue tells you that you have a sense of trust in yourself and your worth then it's time to start dealing – but not before.

● ● ● Tend your fire

Change, according to creativity consultant Robert Fritz, is best achieved by following the process for building a fire. Apply this model to planning your new career deal and it becomes clear that powerful outcomes come from careful tending. You need to start with laying down some kindling. They are those small pieces of inflammable materials which catch light quickly. In career terms they are those easy to do actions which give you a sense of progress: the phone call to a colleague, or the enquiry about a new business area. They are actions which immediately take you a step forward. Kindling soon burns out if that's all there is on the hearth. For the fire to grow you need to start building a structure of larger sticks, just as many career aspirations burn out when the need to build a structure for achieving them is ignored. The attraction of kindling is that it has quick results and gives out large amounts of energy at the start. Building the fire requires giving time to decide the structure that will work best and which of your sticks should be used. Once that structure is in place and a stronger heat is being given out, then larger logs can be added. Those logs are the bigger risks, which you can take once you have confidence that the structure of the fire is firm.

> **"When your inner dialogue tells you that you have a sense of trust in yourself and your worth then it's time to start dealing – but not before."**

The fire that burns best of all is the one which is continuously tended, so that new logs are added according to the emerging shape of the whole, with a log at the top which can guide the fire as to where it should go. As the fire burns, the log on top will fall down and will need to be replaced, or the fire will lose its direction. In the same way each of our careers has to have a log on top: a place for our energy to be directed, or it will burn out. The fire doesn't always have to be large. It can burn low at times and be rekindled at others – but if we ignore the fire in the hope it will take care of itself, or that someone else will mind it for us, we will be disappointed.

The conditions are now right for you to start that fire, for you to build your new deal. Are you ready to strike the match?

references and further reading
● ● ●

A Course in Miracles, Arkana (1985).

Barrett, Gavin (1995) *Forensic Marketing*, McGraw-Hill.

Bridges, William (1980) *Transitions: Making Sense of Life's Changes*, Addison Wesley.

Bridges, William (1995) *Job Shift*, Nicholas Brealey.

Champy James (1995) *Reengineering Management*, Harper Collins.

Cleghorn, Patricia (1995) *Secrets of Self Esteem*, Element Books.

Crainer, Stuart (1995) *How To Have A Brilliant Career Without Ever Having A Proper Job*, Pitman Publishing.

Department of Employment (1995) *Labour Market and Skills Trends, 1995/96*, Skills and Enterprise Network.

EWMD Report on Networking (1994) Sundridge Park Management Centre.

Ferguson, Andrew (1992) *Creating Abundance: How to Bring Wealth and Fulfilment into Your Life*, Piatkus.

Fisher, Roger and Ury, William (1987) *Getting to Yes*, Arrow Business Books.

Fritz, Robert (1994) *Creating*, Butterworth-Heinemann.

GHN Career Management Consultants (1994) *Future Top Managers Report*, GHN.

Guterman, Mark S. (1994) *Common Sense for Uncommon Times: The Power of Balance in Work, Family and Personal Lives*, Consulting Psychologist Press.

Handy, Charles (1989) *The Age of Unreason*, Hutchinson.

Handy, Charles (1994) *The Empty Raincoat*, Hutchinson.

Herriot, Peter and Pemberton, Carole (1993) *Strategic Manager of 2003*, Sundridge Park Management Centre.

Herriot, Peter and Pemberton, Carole (1994) *Competitive Advantage Through Diversity*, Sage.

Herriot, Peter and Pemberton, Carole (1995) *New Deals*, Wiley.

Holbeche, Linda (1994) *Career Development in Flatter Structures*, Roffey Park Research Report.

Jennings, Marie (1992) *10 Steps to the Top*, Piatkus.

Kennedy, Gavin (1993) *Everything is Negotiable*, Arrow Business Books.

MCA (1995) *MCA/FT Management Essays*, MCA, London.

Morin, William J. and Cabrera, James C. (1991) *Parting Company*, Harvest/HBJ Original.

Noer, David (1993) *Healing the Wounds*, Jossey Bass.

Pearce, Jone L. (1994) 'What difference does it make? The psychological involvement of members of a mixed core-periphery workforce', paper delivered at the American Academy of

Management Conference, Dallas, Texas.

Perkins, Graham (1995) *Killer CVs and Hidden Approaches*, Pitman Publishing (1995).

Peters, Tom (1994) *The Tom Peters Seminar: Crazy Times Call for Crazy Organisations*, Macmillan.

Pfeffer, Jeffrey (1980) *Power in Organisations*, Pitman Publishing.

Pfeffer, Jeffrey (1995) *Competitive Advantage Through People*, Harvard Business School Press.

Price, Fiona (1995) *The Shark Free Guide to Financial Advice*, Fiona Price and Partners, London.

Rajan, Amin (1990) *A Zero Sum Game – Business, Know-how and Challenges in an Integrated Europe*, Industrial Society.

Rajan, Amin (1992) 1990's: *Where Will the New Jobs Be?*, Institute of Careers Guidance and Centre for Research in Employment and Technology in Europe.

Ruderman, Marian N. and Ohlott, Patricia J. (1994) *The Realities of Management Promotion*, Center for Creative Leadership.

Scase, Richard and Goffee, Robert (1989) *Reluctant Managers: Their Work and Lifestyles*, Unwin and Hyman.

Sher, Barbara (1979) Wishcraft: *How To Get What You Really Want*, Ballantine Books.

Smith, Bryan and Morphey, Grahame (1994) 'Tough challenges – how big a learning gap', *Journal of Management Development*, 13(8):26–34.

Super, Donald (1980) 'A life-span, life space approach to career development', *Journal of Vocational Behavior* 26:282–98.

Yukl, G. and Falbe, C. M. (1991) 'The importance of different power sources in downward and lateral relation', *Journal of Applied Psychology* 76:416–23.

index
● ● ●